Discovery Leadership

A Leader's Game Plan for Success

Discovery Leadership
Copyright © 2020 by Discovery Leadership Team, LLC

All rights reserved. No part of this work may be reproduced, stored in a retrieval system or transmitted in any form by any means, electronic, mechanical, photocopying, recording, or otherwise, without written permission of the publisher.

For rights and permissions, please contact:

Discovery Leadership Team
525 Keller Road
Temple, TX 76504
discoveryleadershipteam@gmail.com

ISBN: 9798667998013

10 9 8 7 6 5 4 3 2 1

Jeremy would like to thank God, his Wife and loving family for their continued support.

Contents

Why I Wrote Discovery Leadership 9
Introduction 13

Confronting Fear 16
Comfort Zones 18
Failure is not an option – It is pretty much guaranteed! 24
Understanding Fears 30
Moving Beyond Obstacles 36

Embracing Discovery 40
Early Lesson 42
Bosses & Leaders 46
A New Door 51

Building Your Toolbox 54
Invest in Multiple Tools 56
The Illusion of Power 63
The Influential Leader 67

Grow Your Team 70
Man in the Mirror 72
Balanced Teams 78
Becoming Unnecessary 84

Game Plans 90
Starting Out 92
The Building Process 99
Expanding Roles 117
Tasking to Leading 123
Systems Build Satisfaction 127

Inspired Team Meetings 132
Progressive Meetings 134
Small Wins & Big Accomplishments 144

Master Craftsman 147
Know your craft 149
The Chess Master 155
The Professor 161
Leadership Shadow 167
Final Discovery 171
About the Authors 173
Online Resources to continue your path 175

Why I Wrote *Discovery Leadership*

'Give a person a fish, you feed them for a day; Teach a person how to fish, you feed them for a lifetime.'

I think it follows that a similar idea can be said about leadership. Tell a person how to manage, they will be a manager all their lives, teach a leader how to discover their influence, genius, and emotional intelligence and they will create a leadership shadow for generations to follow.

No matter what your current job or skill level is, it is my sincere hope that Discovery Leadership offers you a path to find a new mindset and skills. We all have strengths that will make us great leaders in our own, unique way. I believe that if you find the courage to open some new doors in your mind, you will find a variety of very important tools to use on that journey.

This book will help you find the best version of yourself through your own path of personal discovery. Although many of the stories reflect my own journey, you will be able to relate some of your own life-changing moments through the lens of your own experience.

Many moments in your life will inspire, motivate, and encourage you to discover the talented individual inside of you. This discovery will allow you to help those around you. We live in a world that needs innovative leaders. It is important that we find those who know how to nurture the new generation of team leaders who are craving reliable systems and a culture of inclusion and growth. The old ways - a rigidly structured corporate ladder where role players are valued over unique contributors are quickly falling away. Progressive ideas that are inclusive, tailored to the individual, and focused on building a diverse team are the new benchmarks for personal and company success.

There is power in discovery. This book will help you unlock that power while giving you a game plan for building a system around you that stimulates development. It is time to dispel the idea that we can simply buy talent. We must foster the growth of all people to become great leaders.

The ideas are laid out to be approachable to many different types of people. You may be a young adult preparing for your first career path, a first-time manager who may or may not have had a comprehensive training, or a veteran leader who continues to see similar obstacles. You may already be an upper level leader looking to inspire the team you support. No matter where you are on your journey, this book celebrates the opportunity to find the talents that make you valuable.

In short, Discovery Leadership is using moments of challenge in your life to discover what is fundamentally important to you and shape your belief system. It is finding a voice and message in your communication with others in the workspace. The process of discovering your talents, fears, and patterns of behavior forms the foundation of your leadership style.

Our mission as leaders is to first discover who *we* are, and then we can begin to understand what all it takes to be a leader. Mihaly Csikszentmihalyi described this journey best:

"One must first embark on the formidable journey of self-discovery in order to create a vision with authentic soul."

We talk a lot about courage and taking the first steps. I had to open that door and solve my challenges too, because giving up is simply not going to help me accomplish my dreams. That is what I want to share with you. If you have found comfort in complacency – maybe you have been unemployed for a while, and it feels safe. Maybe the COVID-19 pandemic took your job, like it did mine, and you are looking for a new path. Maybe you grind it every day at a job but do not push yourself beyond punching the clock. As you navigate each chapter, some things will ring very true to your current situation, while others may seem distant from your present role. I hope you can come back at different times in your life and take a new idea away each time. There are a few movies that I have watched dozens of times, and it never ceases to amaze me how I can spot something new or be impacted by a different part of the story with each new viewing.

I am confident you will be able to see how the practices and examples in this book can benefit you in real time. Even if you only take one or two of the tools presented into practice, it will be one step forward from where you began. Beyond that, the chapters in this book are expanded in our online platforms, with in-depth descriptions, downloadable forms, and immersive content. Look for the QR codes throughout the book and use your **smartphone camera** or **QR Reader app** to follow us online.

In this way the lessons of this book are accessible to different learning styles. Whether you get better results from reading, watching, or listening, our campaign is designed to provide you with an extensive set of tools and resources to make use of the skill set that you are working on.

The theme of this book is Discovery – who you are, who your team members are, and using some simple systems to create greatness. These systems can be applied to multiple industries and seek to embrace leaders in every walk of life. My only request is that if you take something from this book that works well for you, be sure to share and teach others wherever you can.

Introduction

I want to tell you about who I am, and the path that inspired me to share my experiences and lessons learned.

I grew up in a small military town where the biggest thrill was Friday Night Lights. Like many other kids my age in Killeen, Texas, my brave father was overseas for a lot of my school years fighting for our country while my mother worked two jobs while supporting my brother and I in school and extracurricular activities. This pushed me to gravitate towards the charismatic people at my high school. I was very comfortable in that space – it had all the people I liked, teachers that I truly looked up to as leaders, and it gave me an opportunity to participate in group events that made me feel like I was giving something back to my community.

I played several sports, and as a young kid looking to make his way in the world, I think the structure and team effort resonated with who I was. In my early adulthood, I would look to return this feeling by starting my career as a teacher and a coach.

My real passion in these formative years was being a student mentor. In my school it was called the PAL program. I was inspired by the teachers who encouraged me to use my voice in a new way. In preparing for my first interaction with one of the students at a local elementary school, I read up every detail I could about my new PAL, so that I could form a real connection by speaking to them on their terms. Something about helping my peers and incoming students cross a bridge made me feel whole. It was addicting.

Even through college, I continued to participate in peer mentoring programs and team sports. I kept a few jobs in the retail and restaurant world while I studied, and I really liked the idea of having a workspace that relied on a team and family coming together. After graduation, I could not leave that feeling behind – and in my first 'real job' I took a position as a high school teacher and coach in Houston.

Now, coming along for the ride was my beautiful wife. She supported and encouraged me to follow my passions in life. Together we started to build a family. In a twist of fate, on my 25th birthday, she threw me a surprise birthday party at a Main Event location. It was full of video games, laser tag, and had a full restaurant and bar. People were having a blast in every direction. I had seen those giant buildings before but had never been inside of one.

For that entire day we were all in complete awe. There was something so interesting to me about that environment – the energy, the people, the scale of it all. I was still thinking about my experience a few weeks later, and on a whim, I thought I might go talk to them about what it would be like to work there. The interview process was different from anything I had experienced in my jobs up to that point – these folks were high energy and managed huge resources with hundreds of people at every unit.

At 25, I looked across the dinner table at my now 8-months pregnant wife, and we talked about the future. She was so passionate about her small startup business, and we wanted to prioritize her being able to stay home with the new baby, at least for the first year. The opportunity to do both financially and chase this newfound and exciting path was a perfect solution.

I wanted to bring the concept back to my hometown community in central Texas, but I was going to have to learn the ropes as an operator first. At the end of the school year, I left teaching high school for the last time; yet it would not be the last time I used my teaching and coaching to develop new leaders.

I

Confronting Fear

KEY GOALS IN THIS CHAPTER

- *Each opportunity for personal reflection ends with a decision to challenge your ideas of what you are capable of – your personal limits are continually pushed.*

- *As a leader, your role is to drive your team beyond their comfort zone in order to make development happen.*

- *All your goals sit just outside of your comfort zone, and you must use courage to go to that place.*

Comfort Zones

The truth is, today's companies do not pay for the safe person who will simply do a job, they look for someone who dares to be bold and can lift them beyond the current plane. Corie Barry, the first female CEO of Best Buy has had unprecedented success in the company which led to her rise to the top. Along the way she changed and challenged the company strategies, and Best Buy has seen results because of her foresight. In a recent interview she said,

"It's important to make yourself uncomfortable, those are the moments that cause you to grow; but it will also differentiate you the most for the rest of your career."

The last sentence is powerful to me. Without being too direct, she notes that those who stay in their comfort zone blend in with the masses. When you are in your comfort zone, there is nothing special, no sparkle, shine, or skill that separates you from the pack. However, when you venture past this place of comfort you shine differently, you speak differently, you think differently, and you lead differently.

I will be sharing with you a series of tools that I use daily to push my team out of the status quo. I challenge them to stretch themselves and the team to heights they did not see before. Every challenge that you meet outside of your comfort zone causes your vision and life to expand as you see more of what is personally obtainable. Each test destroys the limits of how far you think you can go.

Comfort can make you feel safe and secure. It can allow you to feel like you are in control. However, the reality is that at any moment something could come along and knock you out of that safe space. I am not advocating for daily drastic and life-altering challenges, but you should live each day with a moment that challenges your perception of living easy.

The ESPN series "The Last Dance" gave us a behind-the-scenes look at the Chicago Bulls under the reign of Michael Jordan. He was incredibly dedicated to his craft and I appreciated the theme of pressure, how he constantly pushed his team to improve. There was always a feeling of uneasiness, even on the practice court with Jordan. He demanded excellence and demanded that his teammates be the best versions of themselves in practice, so when game time came, they were ready.

While this method is extreme, it cannot be denied that Michael Jordan made everyone on that team better. He pushed them outside their comfort zone to help them enhance their own abilities. His legacy of accomplishment during his time with the Bulls speaks for itself.

We also have clear evidence that points to what happens in the absence of that driver. When Michael Jordan left to play baseball, the team admitted that they all felt a little relief. Not having to push harder than they wanted to, they were able to live in their comfort zone over the next two years. Not surprisingly, the Bulls were not contenders for the title that year or the next, despite being the three-time champions at the start of the season. Comfort is great in theory, but all our true wants and desires are not in our comfort zone, they remain just outside of it.

It is easy for me to take inspiration from my wife and her ability to balance so many things in a day. She works from home and does a phenomenal job of raising our kids, staying on top of our goals, and driving her personal tumbler business. She is very passionate about her tumbler business and we discuss strategy and opportunities all the time.

We were talking about how many people in this sales channel have done well and have been able to take care of their families during COVID-19 with the sales from their tumblers, sometimes even after losing their primary income. I asked her if she thought she could ever get to that level, and she responded that it would be very hard, especially with the kids and the house to take care of. I challenged that thought by asking her about a different situation – if she were a single parent, could she make it work?

As much as that thought was uncomfortable for both of us, the truth is that she would absolutely make it happen. If it ever came to that level, she could close that gap with no hesitation. There would be no time for excuses or for a 'wait and see' mentality. Her desire to see our kids live without needs would be more important than staying in a comfortable mindset.

When we stay in our comfort zone, we never see how great we can be, or how talented we truly are. Our gifts are there but like a muscle they need to be forced into action to grow. Pushing yourself out of your comfort zone allows you to strengthen this muscle.

Look at your current situation and really take an honest inventory of your current risk. If you are staying in a space because it is comfortable, what do you have to lose by going outside that comfort zone forever? Then think about what you have to gain. Personal advancement, mastering new skills, building a new level of responsibility all take effort. Often this effort is outside of your current level of comfort.

While it sounds so nice to 'stay grounded,' you do not get to fly with the eagles when your feet are planted firmly on the ground. Your talents and passions may never come to fruition and you will not see the world from a higher point of view. As a word of warning, if you spend your valuable time living in the comfort zone, eventually you will be looking back and wishing you would have pushed for more when you had the opportunity to do so.

Think forward in time, to one year from today. You currently have the choice of two vastly different states to be in when you get there. One is the – "Oops, I did not do anything differently and I'm still stuck in the same spot" that will lead to regret.

In the other space you are a changed person – you don't really feel the pains of the sweat and effort from the challenges you faced, in fact, you're a lot stronger and more tolerant to the things that happen on a daily basis now. You have hit some small milestones and maybe crossed a big goal or two off your list. You feel a sense of pride and growing self-worth.

Although we must live in the present, I think about a cherished John Maxwell passage:

"An infant is born with a clenched fist; a man dies with an open hand. Life has a way of prying free the things we think are so important"

When we stay in our comfort zones our hands are closed shut and we miss out on opportunities to challenge ourselves and each other. We must have an open hand and reach out toward the goals that will bring us satisfaction.

KEY GOALS IN THIS CHAPTER

- *You accept that you could fail, but also guarantee that you will learn from those failures and become stronger.*
- *It is important to earn those scars and understand where they came from*
- *Courage cannot be gifted to you; it is an action that you must initiate on your own.*

Failure is not an option – It is pretty much guaranteed!

> *"We must re-frame failure as a learning tool. We have fallen in love with this idea that we can control our lives and therefore resisting and concerning ourselves with failure. Just like age, the battle of failure is a lost cause and courageous people understand this all very well, which allows them to leap."* -Robert Dyner

If you can acknowledge and confront your own fear of failure, you are ready to Discover how to transfer this new understanding into personal action. You will identify how to coach your teams to that same realization and start getting results.

As kids we had many scars. I can almost guarantee everyone reading this came home from the playground with a busted lip, a nasty scrape, or a few band-aids. Did that ever stop us from being kids? Absolutely not. Skinned knees and all, we adapt to our situations, analyze the results, and learn our boundaries. Kids seem to always push the boundaries, but in my mind that is a natural part of discovery.

At 12 years old, I experienced Fear in a way that was very real. One night I was woken at 2 a.m. from noise outside my family's second story apartment. I then became aware of the sound of the fire alarm. Soon my mother burst in the door telling me to get out.

As she went to wake my brother, I walked through the front door into the apartment hallway. The wave of heat, light, and noxious gas hit me in a way that I had never experienced before. The next sensation was adrenaline and fear in its purest state. My legs seemed completely frozen.

With a tug on the wrist, I finally managed to move down the stairs and out of harm's way. We watched from the parking lot as the flames spread through the other buildings. My closest friend lived below us, and I was suddenly aware of his absence. We were relieved to see him plunge through a cloud of smoke and emerge from his apartment.

However, he was not fearful, he had a purpose. Catching his breath, he rushed back into the smoke and flames to rescue his mother who was still trapped inside. He was barely able to get her out of the apartment in time and collapsed from inhalation on the doorstep.

This 12-year-old version of myself had just experienced paralyzing fear and witnessed someone who had been brave enough to make decisions beyond the fear that he was also experiencing. The fire and flames were not different for either of us, but our actions on that day could not have been more different.

Fast forward eight years. I am in my college dorm room and my roommate has a frying pan on the stove. We are completely distracted by the last few minutes of a bowl game on TV. It only took a whiff of the black smoke pouring out of the kitchen to know that something was terribly wrong, the flicker of flames crawling up the walls and across the ceiling verified it.

My mind immediately went back to that moment in my childhood apartment. However, I was not frozen this time. They say time slows down when your adrenaline is rushing. As I ran out the front door of the dorm room, I remembered the Fire Extinguisher tucked below the cabinet next to the stove.

I turned back into the dorm room, back into the kitchen. In one move, I pulled the pin on the fire extinguisher and was able to subdue the flames. The kitchen and dorm apartment were a total loss, but the damage had been contained and no one was injured. I had coupled split-second decision making with my prior experience with Fear to make the outcome less devastating than it could have been.

I share this with you because this is what fear of failure looks like. The results are always better than the fear that came before. That is not to say every outcome will be the one you wanted, but once you have failed – you failed! Now, figure out how to get back up and do it better the next time. If you succeed, fantastic. The pure joy you feel from *just doing* is an amazing feeling.

> Most kids do not worry about the opinion of others and this allows them to blossom as they discover the world. However, as we become adults, we can become prisoners of worry and judgment from others. This prevents us from releasing the best versions of ourselves and truly discovering the talent that is inside of us.

Either result builds a foundation for you to learn, grow, and improve. You must be mentally strong enough to understand that failures will happen. However, think of them like scars. They leave a mark on your body, but you can always point to them and tell a story that serves as a reminder of a time when you acted with courage. They no longer hurt us nor affect us, but they do give us something to remember as we continue to evolve and grow. Scars can be full of pain, but the way you respond dictates the reverence in which you look at that scar.

Being courageous is a one-handled door that can only be opened from inside of you. No matter how much external forces inspire you, only you can step into courageousness.

The most compact summation of this idea comes from the impressive perspective of the late Eleanor Roosevelt:

"Do one thing every day that scares you."

We must be aware of this in our own actions, and how we interact with and support our team leaders. No matter what your current level is in the business, you are probably looking up to your superiors for validation. Realize that those underneath your guidance and leadership desire to have your approval also.

There are only a few things that I really preach to my newest leaders, and I think you need to hear the same speech. Small steps forward will not take you very far at first but learning to get past obstacles will build courage. When you get to that place where you can forego fear and start taking big steps there will be much bigger obstacles. If you have built that toughness and endurance, the reward will be far greater than you could have ever imagined when you took that first small step.

KEY GOALS IN THIS CHAPTER

- *Simply understand that you will face fears. Your ability to confront the first challenge with action will open the door to many more lessons and successes.*
- *What is the basis for fear? Can you challenge your own beliefs about why you are feeling fear?*
- *To choose action guarantees that you will learn a new lesson, whether you succeed or not. Failing to act delays your timeline indefinitely.*

Understanding Fears

My first assignment with my new job at Main Event came and my wife and I ended up moving to Austin. I had no clue what I was doing in a 75,000 square foot building filled with video games, laser tag, and rock climbing – however, I had a phenomenal leader and mentor in a guy named Steve Jackson. I sure needed that support. Between my lack of management experience, industry experience, being the new guy and inherited problems inside of the building, it is easy to say that I needed someone to help me maintain my confidence. Day one as a manager was tough. Just in training, I had written down a list of all the things that were going to be learning opportunities for me.

- New to inventory
- Leading people. These were not kids, but adults with bills to pay
- Learning to lead by example – it felt like I was always 'on stage'
- Figuring out the flow of business – employees, guests, and vendors
- Profit and Loss Statements, and how to manage costs
- How to handle guest interactions
- Working with a team on different levels, each with their own agenda
- Learning to control my own emotions in a high stress environment

You may be in my same situation, but in a different building or different industry. It is a regular thing for young, driven management candidates to get thrown into tough situations just to see if they can hack it. Ultimately, they earn their stripes by paying their dues. This is a flawed but prevalent strategy because the mindset is to see if a candidate will sink or swim before the investment in leadership development happens.

I had a colleague who did not say anything to new managers until 3 months in. He wanted to see if they would cut it before he put any energy into their path. I would say that this approach to new leaders can lead to lost respect, turnover on real talent, and increased self-doubt. Being mindful of the experiences of others, especially new people on your team, will make a lasting impact on how they perceive you. Your impact on their first day is very similar to a child taking their first steps – establishing a basis of trust, support, and developmental coaching is what will allow them to grow with you.

Here is an important part of Discovery. Consider the emotions and experience of a brand-new employee walking into your building. Imagine that they were given a survey after their first day to reflect specifically on what they thought of your interactions on that day. Would their experience reflect your desired leadership style?

Back to Week One for me. I was ready to hit the ground running. I had no tools, no bearings, but I did have endless ideas on how to fix the issues in my department. I was nervous to say the least, and then this terrible concept of fear of failure crept in my brain. What had I gotten myself into? I had just moved halfway across the state and could potentially fall flat on my face if I could not start putting the pieces together right away.

I remember overthinking and overanalyzing my first move to the point that Steve had to pull me in the office. I am grateful for the pep talk he gave me:

"Stop overthinking things and just do it, Jeremy. if you mess up, so what? We correct it and move on. As long as your intentions are pure you have my full support."

Flash back to my memories of coaching ball at the high school. Many times I had challenged kids with the same simple advice:

"Go full speed! If you make a mistake going full speed, I can accept it, but if you are half-stepping you will see me on the sidelines."

I once read a passage about the origins of fear. What makes our brain do this thing that absolutely prevents us from taking another step forward? Why is that mechanism in place? There is one thought experiment that I draw on when I think about fear of failure. This can benefit anyone who is having difficulty taking the first step into whatever it is that they want to do.

I imagine a caveman sitting in his cave around a small campfire – slowly and ominously a shadow grows on the wall of a saber-toothed tiger walking into his area.

That chemical reaction in the brain and the rush – that is the fear. If you do not run away from this threat *right now*, it will probably kill you. The root cause of fear is your brain trying to keep you from dying. Not a whole lot in our Neanderthal brains has changed since then, but the things that we interpret as fear are dramatically different from those caveman days.

For example, many people, myself included, build up so much anxiety and pressure at the thought of having to speak in public. The trick I came up with to deal with this is simple. I ask myself, "Will this KILL you, Jeremy?" And at that point, I have become aware of the trick that my own brain was trying to pull on me. I can openly defy the request of fear because I have identified it for what it was posing to be.

Fear of failure is a real thing AND a fake thing all in one. It is a real concept that holds our best version of ourselves prisoners to a premise that we will fail. We unjustly prison our best thoughts, ideas, and versions of ourselves because we are worried about an outcome that *has not actually happened*. I had to confront my own fear of failure and start taking action. These conversations with Steve became the reflecting pool for me to see my own shortcomings and became another step on my path of personal Leadership Discovery.

I cannot express how valuable and formative it was to just be able to talk through my issues with people who had already walked through my path. Thankfully, Steve was the role model for the definition of leadership by allowing me to discover on my own. I trusted him because he shared even his own personal failures with me in an open and honest dialogue. When I think about my coaching sessions in my current world, I know I have Steve to thank for being a master of this skill.

Each obstacle, opportunity, or idea will present to you a chance to act. Considering the choices, two eventualities are certain.

First, should you choose to take action, you will be rewarded with new knowledge and perspective. Whether you earn a scar from failure or a new expansion of what you thought was possible in success, you can now teach and mentor another person who is about to embark on a similar decision.

If you fail to act, you forego the acquisition of knowledge. You cannot see the path any clearer, you have kept your vision limited to what you already know, and you cannot effectively teach or coach another team member who is facing the same challenge.

KEY GOALS IN THIS CHAPTER

- *You are ready to start on the path of Discovery, ready to dive in and DO Something.*

- *You remember that every discovery leads to better decisions. Never fail the same way twice.*

- *You can acknowledge that every action, no matter how big or how small, creates the opportunity to be a subject matter expert, and then a coach and mentor in the future*

Moving Beyond Obstacles

Remember Steve's advice that I should just go for something? Soon after that initial pep talk, I went back to his office and rattled off dozens of items I wanted to do. I wanted to move the furniture around, have a server selling contest, discount a featured item, and so on. Despite his guidance to try things, he would still coach me on whether he thought an idea was worth my investment. He would simply say "Nope, won't work, or maybe." He would smile and say, "Try again next week rookie."

Although it might seem like he was stifling my newfound motivation, it was a very effective strategy to teach me about focusing my decision-making process. Steve was supportive of me trying new things and encouraged me to fly. However, he also wanted to make sure that I was on a path that would lead me to my destination and not into the woods. Often, we have an idea and since it is our idea, we believe it to be excellent. Obtaining a mentor's perspective can help you see some gaps or areas you need to strengthen before you move forward. That is exactly what Steve did for me. Have you ever had a plan that seemed bulletproof, only to end up being a train wreck when executed? I have, and that is why Steve's guidance was an important step in my discovery process.

That week, coming out of the office, I smiled too. I was still ambitious, and tried almost all my terrible, mediocre, and good ideas with Steve's blessing so I could see how they worked. Just like any other workspace I had other managers around telling me they had tried the same thing and it did not work. They laughed at me and were judgmental because I was doing something they had tried and failed to accomplish. They wanted me to accept their failures without explanation or going through the process myself.

I discovered so much during that time. Some items I was able to do at a high rate, others they were right about, but the experience of going through and building a foundation for myself on best practices that I could later fully explain was the most important part of that process. Steve was the ultimate leader and never wanted me to do what the average person would or would not do. He was the coach who encouraged creativity, innovation, and energy. He allowed me to be free and try as much as I wanted without ever judging me, just simply coaching and guiding.

I met with him the next week, and my ideas went from 100 nos to one good idea. When I found success, I was able to come back each week with even more concrete items that won both his approval and the approval of my leadership team. Over time, he showed me how to make great decisions, waste less time on trivial ideas, and find support from both my leaders and the team of managers and employees around me. Through my small wins they began to see me as a leader and not just a rookie learning the ropes. They began supporting my ideas and my successes started to pile up.

The valuable lesson here is that even though I started with 100 nos, I could see for myself what effect it had on my team. This led me to discover the "why" behind Steve's nos. Every mistake I made helped me to find the source of why something did not work, how to make small changes to an idea to get it to work, and why sometimes Steve completely rejected my idea. I had to go through this discovery process to truly understand the path he was taking me through.

Parents want to help their own kids avoid the mistakes they made growing up but doing so all the time deprives them of discovering life lessons for themselves. Let that sink in. If a person is not allowed to fail sometimes, how can they learn to be successful? The moments I had under Steve allowed me to try every good, bad, and crazy idea.

One year later, I found myself confident in making good decisions. I had closed many of the gaps in knowledge I identified that first week. I had invested in my own discovery and worried little about potential failures, laughs, or judgments. Many of my creative ideas were adopted throughout the company, and I was tremendously proud. Discovery was the key to my success; without those lessons and freedom I would not have been able to excel.

You may be in a situation where your current supervisor or leader does not give you the same space that Steve did for me. The important thing to do is hold on to your values and build up wins where you can. With some people, trust and freedom are earned, and require a history of success stories before they can feel comfortable with expanding your role. My advice in that situation is to keep an open line of communication and try to celebrate even small wins when they happen.

The other half of this equation has to do with priorities. On any job, there are things that need to get done daily, and things you may want to get done. Getting good at the basics of your job description is a prerequisite to doing the creative things. Do not skip the basics. In fact, "Know Your Craft" is an entire discussion in Chapter 7 of this book.

One of my best friends has this philosophy *"Whine now and enjoy later,"* meaning you may have to work hard on the mechanics for the first few months of a new project, but once a system is in place you get to enjoy the results.

II

Embracing Discovery

KEY GOALS IN THIS CHAPTER

- *You cannot teach others until you have collected your own set of scars.*
- *Each experience should give you a chance to reflect*
- *If you had to do the same task twice, you should never fail the same way twice*

Early Lesson

Being young and ambitious, you sometimes run into barriers and must learn to channel that energy correctly. I think about an experience in my young life where ambition and energy left me with a literal black eye.

Between high school graduation and college football tryouts, a friend recommended I should try training at the local boxing gym to get my strength and cardio up. With some great trainers, I went into it 100%, working on the basics of footwork, hand speed, and tactics every single day. About a month into this, my coach challenged me to stop hitting bags and start sparring against a real opponent.

My first sparring match was three rounds. I did not want to look like an idiot, as I had never done anything like this before. My heart was pounding, my mind was racing, and my nerves were shot. My legs felt like Jell-O as everyone in the gym gathered around. When the bell rang, I could barely move. But then I took the first step. Drawing on all my technical training and daily practice, I threw my first punch. In one moment, I thought I had conquered my fears. That was reversed in a split second when I got my first punch right to the stomach.

He followed with a right to the head, left to the body and then another left to my head. In a moment all fear and nerves were lost, pure anger came out. I sent a flurry of punches his way with no strategy, no discipline, and most importantly with zero control of emotions.

My opponent sat back and analyzed my style. and in a matter of seconds was able to use his skill and put me on my back side. When that emotion took over, I ignored all my training and tactics, and paid the price. In between rounds, I had to take a quick inventory of what had just happened and figure out what needed to happen next.

I was still a little nervous as I went back into the ring, but more focused. I began by allowing the opponent to hit me first and allow me to understand his style. I wanted to channel that anger into focus, timing, and strategy. The opponent that had very recently put me on my backside had to get ready for a better version of me, because I had learned from the experience of letting my emotions dictate my behavior.

In a very real sense, this experience formed the basis of the system I now call Discovery Leadership. Although we might not all live and work in a boxing ring, we train and practice every day. You do not get to truly know how you will respond, act out, and participate until you have done a lot of self-exploration. Those moments of sitting in the corner are repeated for me every time I have a challenge at work. How can I use the skills I have, inside of me, to get the result I want instead of getting punched in the face again?

KEY GOALS IN THIS CHAPTER

- *I can respond as a boss, but this will not build a team. I can respond as a Leader, and the team will grow around me.*

- *If you are focused on becoming a great leader, you will first analyze the role you own in all your personal relationships.*

- *Be cautious of which lessons you choose to mimic. Leaders can role model positive methods as well as negative ones.*

Bosses & Leaders

My team had made some real steps forward, and I was asked to transfer to another new location so that I could help change the culture and develop some strong leaders who needed just a little fine tuning. I was honored for the opportunity, as it would give me a chance to verify that my new systems were working.

In the past year I had traveled through one layer of self-doubt and was ready to inspire my team to do the same. I wanted to give them the opportunity to discover their strengths, guide their decisions, and become promotable through good leadership skills. A singular method of thinking had brought me success so quickly, I wanted nothing to change. Similarly, I hoped my new boss would continue to do the same for me. However, that is not what transpired. My new boss had a completely different set of ideals and management style.

His focus was on all the little things and it seemed like the details were more important than the big picture. Instead of praising an inspirational meeting, he would point out that a trash can had a dirty spot on it. Instead of having detailed teaching moments he would send an email with a list of things he saw wrong. He coached in fear of confrontation, which was demoralizing to the team and had us all running in circles.

I was frustrated with the type of daily communication he put into my inbox that had no growth value. To work hard and feel as if nothing I could ever do would be good enough weighed me down and I forgot my motivations of being a leader. It was very similar to that gut punch; I could not see past my emotions to really discover a path to be a better person.

No matter how badly I wanted to advance into a regional leader, I could not come to terms with adapting to his different leadership style. Yet this made me discover a whole new thought about what I wanted out of my own interactions with my leadership team.

An ideal leader cannot forget they have dual roles. First, they must be the head coach. That means making the decisions, creating game plans, having personal development moments, driving the team to success, and pushing them to new goals. Even the best players on a team need a coach, and there is no way to avoid this part of the job.

A leader must also be a cheerleader. All people need to feel supported and encouraged. Often it is perceived as a weakness to celebrate those working for you. However, tell me the last time a compliment made you feel bad. Was there a time when words of pure encouragement did not excite you? If you saw someone jumping up and down in support of you, would you get mad and tell them to stop? Many people list positive praise as one of their primary motivators at work. Money alone is rarely enough to keep folks going and does not encourage them to do more.

At this junction in my career, I was eager for another challenge, and it was apparent that there would be many more years of investment in this company before I was going to have a shot at moving up. I had many conversations with my peers and family to help me find a path to advancement.

Despite all my recent success and the pride I had in my now growing team, a new challenge with a growing concept had caught my eye. The opportunity to learn a new skill set, utilize my new leadership strengths, and be a foundational part of a very fast-moving company was simply too much to pass up.

Being young and immature also kept me from simply having an open conversation about my feelings, thoughts, and desires with my boss, which I regret. The importance of open communication cannot be underestimated. I want to share with you a simple exercise to try and identify a way to close gaps in communication and lead you to an action that will be productive instead of reactive. If you would like to use this example as a team exercise, or to write out answers without tearing a page out of the book, you can follow the resource link through the chapter QR code or via the link at the end of the book.

If I could say one thing to my boss's face and he could not retaliate, what would I say?

What is the root cause of your frustration?

Put yourself in your supervisor's position. What about your relationship with them could cause this rift?

What is one step you could personally take to get closer to improving your frustrations?

Take ownership, know that you must be the agent of change. Say aloud the following sentence:

"I need your help with a problem I am having..."

Thinking of all you have written down above, what is the next thing you would say?

KEY GOALS IN THIS CHAPTER

- *You cannot simply run away from issues that you do not want to deal with.*

- *Impossible challenges come up when you do not have the vision to get around them, or if you have not challenged yourself to make a bold move to learn a new lesson.*

- *Become a teacher who focuses on the details, do not stop just because the lesson is over. Creating a problem list without offering the 'why' does not empower your team to build their skill set.*

- *Having the perspective of your experience and scars is what you will use to guide a team through their own personal path of discovery.*

A New Door

I decided to take a new leap of faith. This time I had the mindset and skills to really deliver a new system. My personal challenge included learning a new concept, a dinner-movie cinema, with a young and growing leadership team. However, the new company did not owe me anything career-wise. Not to mention I had no idea how a movie theater even worked, outside of how to butter my popcorn.

When I arrived in my new career path, I came to realize that the universe has a funny way of making sure you get past the important obstacles. This time, I recognized the scars I already had, and knew some personal growth would be required for me to excel in this new role.

Even after several years in a management role, I still had not learned the communication skills to avoid getting frustrated with the personality traits of my old boss. Sure enough, my new leader Scott was the same guy but with a lot more intensity. I had unwittingly arrived in a culture with a high energy boss focused on over-communication and an obsession with detail, just in a new building.

There remained one critical difference, which would be a key to my next level of Discovery on my path. Scott had a knack of being able to break down and explain every decision he made, and never broke away until he was confident that I had understood the "Why".

I remembered back to a time when I knew nothing about the entertainment industry. I had to scrape my knees to learn every single lesson. Finding a leader who took time to paint the picture in exquisite detail was a much less painful way to learn the business. I began to enjoy and appreciate the over explanation of even the simplest of things – it seemed like each day I was becoming a subject-matter expert on something new. To close that knowledge gap so quickly allowed me to make better hiring choices, train better, and help make critical business decisions with greater accuracy. I had grown as a teacher, and my challenge to lead had also grown. This was not about being green and full of energy anymore, it was about making better decisions.

Scott was brilliant, confident, and intense. He demanded a lot out of the team and challenged me in ways that I had never been challenged before. I never wanted to fall short of his personal standard because he would always ask that dreaded question. "Now Jeremy, walk me through your thought process here..."

> *Gemba Walk*
>
> An opportunity for leaders to stand back from their day-to-day tasks to walk the floor of their workplace to identify opportunities. The objective of Gemba walk is to understand the places that generate value and identify problems rather than review results or make superficial comments.

Because of the lessons learned already, I grew immensely under his watch. I learned a technique called the "Gemba Walk" where we would walk the building, sharing details and vision of perceived opportunities. We would follow up and educate the team after our observations. He would ask me questions to stem discovery, such as, "How does this align with our core values?" or "Are you adding value or losing guest equity?" From these walks, I learned many lessons and expanded my ability to see opportunities. I learned and accepted his appetite for teaching every detail no matter how many minutes or hours it took to go over one point. It was simply exciting to have a leader coaching my development, and not just managing my tasks. Now, the details had a reason behind them, and I was excited to find ways to bring my building to perfection.

Quickly, I was able to absorb and respect Scott's IQ of the theater business. This taught me how to prepare for the many curve balls that come with daily operations. I discovered how to have attention to detail, a trait that had been missing in my prior life. I thought I had a good work ethic before, but Scott truly challenged me to be a warrior in the workplace and set a new personal standard that everyone saw and respected.

As he was promoted, I followed. This promotion was bittersweet; I was excited to see my diligent work rewarded, but I also knew this time that there was more responsibility coming my way. I had joined the company in the spring, had a crash course over the summer, and was handed the reins in November. Enough time? No, but I knew that my foundation of good decision making, and continued Leadership Discovery would help me find my path from here on.

Perhaps your current assignment will find you with great training, good leaders, and a firm support structure in a learning environment that allows you to stack wins and learn through just doing. In many situations though, you must find a way to grow and become a stronger leader through understanding yourself first. Acknowledge that your growing team leaders need you to speak in detail, not just offer a list of tasks. The challenges ahead are simply milestones that will soon write the story of your successes.

Sometimes it is difficult to understand what your team needs when giving someone a detailed description of a task to complete. Focusing on the importance of detail to guarantee the learner has comprehension is the goal. Painting the picture with more detail means the learner can see what you are saying – this makes direction and instruction easier to follow.

III

Building Your Toolbox

KEY GOALS IN THIS CHAPTER

- *This chapter will help you form a vision statement of what you want your current or future team to become.*

- *Take inventory of your strengths and try to find people who will complement your skill set, not mimic it. Identify bias and actively reject its influence on your decision making.*

- *This is the chapter that you should come back to often as it gives you an opportunity to take a fresh look at the true composition of your leadership team.*

Invest in Multiple Tools

Tom was a stud supervisor in my kitchen who was an absolute beast when it came to cooking, cleaning, organizing, and getting things done. Tom was any manager's dream -- humble, dedicated, honest, and a growing leader in the ranks. He was happy to admit that he was very strict but got a lot of work out of the team. If you were a hard-nosed worker like Tom, you would get along great. If there was any lack of discipline or talking back, the tables turned quickly. He would want to get rid of you and find another person with talent and mold a new person under his wing.

This is certainly a 'method' that exists in the real world. Do not get me wrong, I love watching 'Hell's Kitchen' with Gordan Ramsay, but that methodology has less and less efficacy in today's culture. Ramsay's response to those who are not on the same page is to push them even harder and treat them like the old school chefs -- yelling, demanding, and thinning the team out. There is only one tool in the toolbox – and it is a hammer. Similarly, Tom was completely unable to understand, relate, and engage in the needs of the team. As a side effect, the only leaders who grew in that shadow were similarly one-dimensional.

You must approach each leader on your team differently, because not all people react to things the same way. Many failures from leadership come because they only have one tool to use. They pound and pound without soliciting feedback to understand what the real issue is.

Below are some important methods for connecting with your team, and the idea that each method is like adding a new tool to your personal toolbox. You cannot turn a screw with a hammer. Let us imagine you have a very intelligent team leader, but their defining personality trait is shyness. I highly doubt you could *yell your way to success* with this personality.

We must understand that when we go into a coaching situation with a team leader, guest, or employee, you must have multiple items in your toolbox and be ready to use any one of them depending on the situation. You must start the conversation by listening and asking questions, to discover the best method. Here are some of my favorite tools, although this list is nowhere near exhaustive. It is simply a variety of approaches that I rely on to open good communication without having to resort to pulling out the hammer.

First, assume no knowledge

If I am training a team member on a task, but I have not observed them in that role previously, I start off with the assumption that they have zero experience with the task at hand. This means defining each tool needed, every step of the process, and any tips or tricks I have for getting the desired result. Realize that this does not imply that the learner is without skill, but rather that you have made a mental plan to cover the entire topic in complete detail.

Listening

This is the first tool I reach for in the Discovery phase. I have no greater method of finding out exactly who I am coaching, and what I need to work on to get the desired result.

Seeking to understand

This is a tool focused on active listening. What is your leader saying to you? How can you put yourself into their perspective with deeper understanding? Getting to the root cause, and the "why" will help you shape future decision making and build trust.

Finding individual strengths

I want to seek out what makes each person unique, and more importantly, what can they contribute through passion and innate skill? If you are a strong speaker, I want you leading team meetings. If you are a planner, I want to put you in a place to set up the team for success through task delegation.

Utilize One-on-one meetings

I would guess that more than half of all people are much more comfortable talking about their needs, fears, or challenges in a small group or 1-on-1 setting. Social anxiety, fear of public speaking, pride, and defensive posturing all come off the table when conversations get into a smaller format.

Create daily game plans

Creating a plan each day that empowers your entire team, depending on their unique skill set. Chapter 5 of this book focuses specifically on growing this skill path. Good leaders know their expectations, goals, and the things that must be done every day to feel success.

Asking open ended questions

Open-ended questions can be defined as any question that cannot be answered with a simple Yes or No response. For example, "How did you arrive at that decision?" These questions allow you to step into the mind of your conversational partner, and they offer more than just facts – you also get context. Any question that starts with who / what / why / when / how is typically going to be open-ended.

Removing fear

I want to reward people who live outside of their comfort zone, but who are also willing to take a step back after each experience and analyze what was done – for better or for worse. Providing a nurturing environment that encourages new ideas is the home base of leading without fear. This requires you to reflect on previous decisions without the threat of punishment. If your people fear that honesty will result in something negative happening, you are probably not going to get the real story.

Empowering freedom of ideas

Our culture is diverse, and so too should be our ideas. Small groups, one-on-one conversation, and allowing initiatives to come to life reflect the value and trust I place in leaders who want to develop. If someone comes to you with an idea, your first step should be to schedule a time and place where you can hear it out in its entirety. This also allows you the opportunity to ask for preparation on their behalf, which will help them to self-discover potential pitfalls or more efficient paths.

Sharing the knowledge

No lesson learned should stay private. We can all grow through shared experiences if those lessons become common knowledge. You must have a stable platform for open communication before you see results here. If several of your team leaders are experiencing common problems without finding success, it is time to look at communicating that knowledge in a group setting.

Call them leaders

No matter your job code, name tag, or paycheck, if you are on my team, I need you to lead some facet of the operation. I address my leadership team as just that, and I expect them to do the same to each other. Walking the walk will happen to your team when you mentally change their behavior from just following.

Find a way to praise, everyday

A day without praise is like a day without sunshine. Momentum disappears quickly if I am not driving our team through positive energy and continuing to pay into that system at every single opportunity. Leaders who are seeking praise will act in ways that are praise-worth, just for the thrill of being recognized.

Coach, do not task

If a team leader owns a job, I should not step in to do tasks unless things are absolutely crashing down around them. My best role is in seeing things from a higher perspective, coaching through the struggles, and sharing what I know about planning and processes. My favorite coaching guideline is, if I am working too hard, it is because I did not plan hard enough.

With a little practice any of these tools can be yours. Reflect on which items on my list come through as strengths in your methods. Is there something on this list that you would like to add to your personal inventory? Think about your next opportunity to coach a team member and go after that communication with one of these items on the list. I am certain that if you find the courage to put the hammer away, you will find a different level of success with your team

If you are using the tools of leadership and respect people for their strengths, you will inspire those around you even if you are not titled as their boss. In a contrasting example, getting that promotion or title does not indicate that your methods are better than your subordinates. When you stand for principles and actions that are just, the energy pushing you forward from those that support you will define your role. To be concerned with a paycheck or management title is often a tenuous position that will not offer much satisfaction. On your way up, you will see many people who justify their methods because of their title. Let your leadership define you, and the prize of titles will become so much less important.

KEY GOALS IN THIS CHAPTER

- *If you focus on leading through power, the development stops right there.*
- *Power is rarely earned, it usually comes from title, money, or nepotism.*
- *You can avoid power moves by staying true to the ideals of discovery, and modeling behaviors*
- *Buying talent is expensive and will likely not last long.*
- *A title does not define your leadership style*

The Illusion of Power

Some may say that if you are leading well, the results will follow. In many companies, those results are often measured on a scorecard with multiple categories. There is rarely a category on that scorecard called "quality of leadership." Despite that, I also know that companies want innovators, jolts of electricity, and most importantly, an influencer.

The power of influence is a special trait that appeals to a person through persuasion and relationships. Do not confuse the words 'power' and 'influence' because they mean two completely different things. Power leadership is using your authority to get things done, whereas influence allows you to appeal to the person you are trying to move in a certain direction.

If you reflect on leaders that you have had in the past, I'm sure you can think of someone who asserted leadership through power – "My way or the highway" is a pretty standard expression for a power leader. When things go off the rails a bit, this type of leader can be accused of going on a 'power trip.' Conversely, if you are influenced by someone, it is usually because you look up to them in some form or fashion. Think of someone you know who influenced you in a decision-making process. Whether the decision was a good or bad one, you may have changed your opinion, gone outside of your comfort zone, or made a decision that you would not have made without the belief that their push was in the direction you needed to go.

Now, consider your feelings about each of those personality types. Although there is much to envy about Power, there are significant drawbacks to consistently leading through power moves. Most Influencers are often trying to move everyone in a similar direction through persuasion. What type of leadership traits would you want your team to reflect when they think about your personal leadership style?

Here is an assertion that is hard to refute at face value:

"If you want a high-performing team, simply hire the best people. If they cannot hack it, find better people, and replace them. If you are always replacing the weakest link, then your chain only gets stronger."

I have come across a hiring manager whom I would consider an 'elitist' because he only wanted to hire a bunch of Spartans for his team. It was well known that he looked down on people that were not as talented as he desired, nor would he give people the time of day if they could not get something done. The line was drawn very distinctly - he wanted these people out of his building immediately. In his eyes he only had time for Spartans, the "best of the best".

There are few things about this that we need to explore. First and foremost, when leading an army of Spartans, you do not have to be a great leader or have any developing skills. They are already there. Highly talented, ready for action, and they perform at a high level. You point and they attack. You can lead this team with Power but not influence, which does not warrant a lot of skill. Three things about Spartans: they are incredibly rare, they're not cheap, and they don't last that long. Say what you will about the movie 300, but how many of them made it back to the party in Sparta?

The other part of this equation is that a Spartan leader never gets to say they developed something. The difference in gathering people around you, developing their skills, and finding a common goal is the real reward. Watching people conquer new heights by training every day and advancing their personal standard should be your goal. What good is a leader who never advanced their team through learning, coaching, and discovery? Everybody wants to skip this step because it takes time, planning and patience.

To say you 'made' a Spartan is not usually truthful -- they are born and built through a culture that demands a lot out of them, and you just happened to be in the right time and place to be blessed by their presence. All you must do is manage them.

We often miss our calling when we search for perfect specimens to be our shadow. In all actuality you will never find a group of Spartans. A great leader will develop their team and build an elite group of leaders that have an array of talent. Take the hunchback from the movie 300. Had they found a way to harness this man's pure desire to be a part of this team and found a way to develop his strengths, they would have realized he had a great gift of geography that would have served the Spartans well. No, he was not a person to put on the front lines. A great leader finds a place for all those around them and influences each one to be the best version of themselves for the greater good of the team.

KEY GOALS IN THIS CHAPTER

- *Focusing on influence allows you to share your decision making across a much wider sphere of influence, including to those in positions above you.*
- *Influential leadership is sustainable*
- *Implement a "rising tide lifts all ships" approach*
- *Be the role model for great behaviors - your actions are so valuable that people start to mimic your behavior*

The Influential Leader

The idea of influence can be related to a leader on the battlefield. If a challenge is situated just over the next hill and you go charging over the top, do you have to look back and see if your team is going to follow you?

Only after a series of challenges, each one offering you the opportunity to build the trust and support of your team, can you confidently go after the big goals. If you have not taken the time to make investments in their personal goals and struggles, do not expect anyone to go rushing into your conquests.

Influential leadership is being able to help your team rid themselves of excuses by showing them solutions to the problems they encounter. Leaders must understand a natural human flaw is to come up with an excuse. It is easy, safe, and comfortable to the person making it. They know their comfort zone well, yet the place you are trying to take them is foreign and it involves risk and self-assessment.

Once you realize this and take ownership of it, you can utilize this knowledge to your advantage by helping your team get out of their own way. First, you must be the one who brings them into the fold on day one. This is a good start, but now you must invest the time coaching them up every day. They will not get there if you allow them to continue to make excuses without showing a path around them.

Keep in mind that people will absolutely give up on themselves. One of your most important roles is being there to pick them back up. Superman does not come to sit and talk, he comes to those in immediate distress and uses his skills to solve the problem.

You must be able to read the room and commit to removing any pressure or expectation placed on your team down to zero at a moment's notice. Once that pressure is off, you can talk about how things got to the place where confidence was lost. Then you can use your perspective to show a path or plan to get back on track. If you can acknowledge that the person in front of you is currently going through the process of being scarred, the way you respond to them will change immediately.

The power is in you taking the time developing your team leaders to use your tools in developing your team leaders and their choices. Their decision is going to be their decision, but by giving them the option to be great, you have given them a choice.

Imagine a hypothetical company in which you are tasked to lead a group of four department leaders, who in turn will lead 20 people each in their departments. Each week, you spend 15 minutes describing one of your favorite tools to use and encourage them to also use that method in the specific examples that come up in your workspace.

Over time, you may see your team begin to use the series of tools that you offered up for discussion, and probably also see some new methods that are becoming important. In this very small way, you have not only impacted the job satisfaction of the four members you supervise directly, but also the 80 people working hard in spaces just outside of your direct communication. The expression "A rising tide lifts all ships" is very appropriate for describing how you can lift the experience of many people through influencing effective skills and behaviors.

IV

Grow Your Team

KEY GOALS IN THIS CHAPTER

- *Teachers focus on the details and never stop short of ensuring that their message is understood completely. No matter the lesson, you start with the beginning step, and all processes are completed without confusion or error.*

- *You cannot cheat the process, although it may be expected for you to do so in your role.*

- *Hiring people because you see yourself in them is a counter-productive methodology for building a diverse and well-rounded team.*

- *Your bias will exist whether you accept it or not. Understanding your bias will help you to separate those ideals when talking to future team leaders.*

Man in the Mirror

As you could imagine, when I embarked on my new role, I encountered a whole new set of problems and experiences. As they came my way, I took each failure or accomplishment as a lesson and embraced each discovery moment that encountered. I knew that without them, I would not evolve and become the leader that my company and my team needed. I had also learned that accepting the results were going to be painful sometimes and rewarding other times – but that each day gave me a new chance to do something new and build on my legacy of knowledge.

The movie business is all about cycles. Learning those cycles plays a pivotal role in your potential success. There are big movies, small movies, holidays, staffing expectations, and a whole list of other variables that could make or break a successful week. I was not a big "movie guy" so this was all brand new to me. I took it all in stride with a smile on my face as always.

> *Think about the challenges in your role that are going to be new to you. There are bound to be things that scare you, excite you, and probably some things you did not even realize were going to be challenges. Remind yourself that every new experience only happens once – reflecting on what you could do better will make you successful the second time around.*

Do not be mistaken, we live in a results-oriented business world. My shortcomings were not just for me to worry about. I, too, had a boss, and my performance was a direct reflection on my leader's ability to keep my mistakes from putting a strain on our company. I worked at the number one location in our small, four-unit company, and our projected growth plan of doubling the company size in two years relied heavily on this unit's continued success.

One thing I quickly realized is that Scott expected me to be him. He wanted me to speak like him, act like him, react like him, plan like him, lead like him. However, I was in discovery season, discovering the business, discovering my team, and discovering how to prepare for these situations in the future.

Scott and I developed some friction between us at that juncture in our relationship because he did not truly understand my mechanics as a leader. I was always chipper, whereas he liked to maintain a stern facade. He took my smiles for weakness and a lack of tenacity instead of seeing the passion, focus, and note-taking that was going on behind the scenes.

He wanted me to skip these stages of discovery. Many leaders do. Never forget the process you had to go through to get to mastery. If it has been many years since that first discovery moment, it is easy to forget the mistakes you had to make along the way. It is harder to understand what support your team needs if your assumption is that they already have the scars. Many leaders want to see you as their reflection because their current behaviors, based on subject matter mastery, is all they can remember.

There is a failure in trying to find yourself in others or trying to conform your pupils into a spitting image. Even in the interview process, many leaders are subconsciously looking for characteristic traits that are "just like me" instead of looking at the unique values that make up a person's behaviors, character, and what they will provide for the team you will surround them with.

Do not cheat the process of discovery. These are our foundations for years to come. Rome was built brick by brick and has withstood the test of time because the process of development was not interrupted, rushed, or halfway done. Discovery is a process that is built moment by moment, action by action, and lesson by lesson. Embrace the process, do not rush it.

There is only one you. Leaders must understand they are one of a kind. If you waste time trying to conform people to your "ideal" you could miss out on the beauty and power in developing the talented person right in front of you. They do not need to conform. Rather, you should commit to discovering the potential they have. This is your opportunity to be authentic and reach back into your past and share your scars with your team leader. No matter what they have accomplished, nobody is perfect. This is a moment in which many leaders can show a side of vulnerability. This vulnerability lets team leaders know that you make mistakes and see how you use those mistakes to make better decisions.

Do you ever wonder why history seems to be so full of father/son quarrels? Why did so many historical children grow up with a chip on their shoulder placed there by their parent figures? Many fathers want their sons to have their same interests, beliefs, convictions, drives, and even career path. When they do not see themselves in their sons they can overreact, rush to judgment, or just simply forget to support and guide in crucial moments because they are blinded by the reflection on themselves. An enlightened leader will have the same mentality as a supportive parent – listening, seeking to understand, and allowing you to grow with the strengths and passions that will make you become great.

Think about a time someone has placed unrealistic expectations on you. Have you ever felt like you were not good enough because of how someone else reacted? I want to take you through a thought process that will help you identify your own "like me" bias.

First, who is your favorite sports team?
Think about your team's biggest rival.
For example, if you are a Dallas Cowboys fan, think about the Eagles. If sports are not your thing, think about a person who admires a celebrity or politician you do not like.

Envision a person who supports that rival, picture what that person looks and acts like. It may help to close your eyes for just a second and form an image.

Now, you have built a mental picture of a person who likely has different beliefs, convictions, and life experiences. Do you have any opinions formed about their characteristics, appearance, or motivations? What about their life experiences would cause them to root for your rival? Do you support them in their decision making? Would you trust them to run your business?

In acknowledging this, you can see how "like me" behaviors impact your judgment before even knowing your team leader's composition or skill set.

Think about an interview set up where the person you are interviewing starts off by saying that they support the rival team, or came from a direct competitor company, or despises your favorite TV show. What is your immediate thought? Are you comparing someone else's answer to what you want to hear, or are you listening for the other person's values and strengths?

KEY GOALS IN THIS CHAPTER

- *If this is your first read through the book, or you are not managing a team, this chapter should help you form a vision statement of what you want your team to become.*

- *Take inventory of your strengths and try to find people who will complement your skill set, not mimic it. Identify bias and actively reject its influence on your decision making.*

- *This is the chapter that you should come back to often as it gives you an opportunity to take a fresh look at the true composition of your leadership team.*

Balanced Teams

I want to reflect on a powerful statement I received during a peer coaching session:

> *"Make sure you maximize your strengths, and not focus as much on your weaknesses. Diamonds are not perfectly shaped, but they are valuable. Weaknesses will get better over time, but your strengths will always be what makes you an asset."*

These words shook me because I had always thought that working on my weaknesses would make me a more well-rounded leader. We are told to make sure we are balanced, right? The retort from my peer counselor:

> *"Why would you do that? Your strengths are your strengths for a reason, recognize them, own them, and magnify them."*

A good example of this was my early struggles with the profit and loss statement. I had no clue how to decipher 10 pages of financial gibberish that supposedly determined whether I was a good leader and my potential bonus. However, as a young leader I was not around leaders who had time to teach me about profit and loss statements. Unfortunately, they did not correlate the actions that we did in the building to this critical document. Now, as a General Manager I could not escape the profit and loss statement. I had to learn how to read it with comprehension. I knew I needed to expand my skills.

I read "Accounting for Dummies," asked a lot of questions, and looked back on previous statements to form a basis of understanding. With time, I learned this crucial piece of paper, but to this day profit and loss statements are not my biggest strength.

This is not to say I cannot read the profit and loss statement to navigate the business and make action items. I could describe to you the basics, but I cannot help you master this skill, as I have not mastered it for myself yet. Remember, I did not join the Math Club in high school, I gravitated towards peer mentoring, coaching, and teaching as my passions. Energy and teaching are natural things I do and feel great doing. Perhaps you have an easier time with writing, math, public speaking, planning, delegation, or conversation than I do. To that end, I have continued to excel and grow in these areas that I am passionate about, while learning the functions and mechanics of other areas such as the profit and loss statement that keep me balanced.

You can strengthen your weaknesses, but it is more important to make sure to magnify your strengths. Trying to be a perfect balance of skills is not what makes us unique or our teams strong. The best thing I ever did to get better at P&L accountability was to find the person on my team who loved to dive into the numbers and train the task away. All that time I spent looking at numbers was re-dedicated into doing the things I do best and getting far more results.

Sharing the topic and teaching the few things I knew helped me to get a new perspective. I learned more about P&L from teaching what I knew and listening to another team member's take on the situation.

Too often we are worried about chasing perfection or focused on 'fixing' what we perceive as weakness. When you think about the skills you bring to the table in your current role, what is it about your style that sets you apart? Are there things about your style you see as weaknesses? Think about which one feels more important to focus your personal energy on.

I recently watched four sports legends play a round of golf – two football players and two pro golfers, paired up. Obviously the two golfers were elite because that is their craft. However, I want to point out an observation about the days before they began their round of golf.

Tom Brady is possibly one of the greatest football players of all time and worked tirelessly to get ready for this event. Each day he woke up early, hit the gym, and put in practice rounds with one of the best golf coaches in the game.

Did he play great? It was okay.
Did he challenge the Pros? Not at all.

Although he prepared his butt off for this event, took everything more seriously than the pros, and gave it his best effort, Tom Brady was completely outplayed.

See, golf is not his strength, Football is. No matter how many rounds of practice that morning, or how many coaches he has, he will never be as great as those pro golfers. His strength is in pro football – so while he can improve on his game and make it a little more sound, the reality is that golf will always be a weakness compared to his greatest strength. I think about that in the same way I view coaching and accounting in my professional life.

Here is where you must make the connection to your team leaders: each one of them has a strength, and you must know what that strength is if you are going to help them develop. Finding that strength attribute is your job and an important part of Discovery Leadership. Through your interactions you should be able to fully understand your role and the role of your leaders, including the challenges, goals, and daily struggles associated with their job.

In my experience, most people say, "I need to focus on improving my weaknesses." It is easy to fall prey to what society tells us, and we often think to be the best version of ourselves, we must focus on our weaknesses. For you to grow a team or yourself, you need to believe that the previous statement is a lie.

The power in realizing your strength allows you to see the areas you are not as strong in. A good leader will surround themselves with people who will help fill those voids. It is rarely a good idea to surround yourself with people who are exactly like you, because you will not be able to attack those areas outside of your comfort zone, grow your team's leadership in those areas, or perform across a broad scope of talents and abilities.

Diversity here is key – let us say you learned to juggle as a kid, joined the circus and became a fantastic role player. If one day you became the General Manager of the circus troupe, you let your affinity for juggling dictate your hiring decisions. Soon, you had a circus full of talented jugglers. Yet what good is a circus with only one act? Different skills and unique contributions is what builds strength and longevity to any team.

It is time to change your mindset – instead of viewing them as liabilities, understand that weaknesses are simply not your biggest asset. That does not mean you should not be aware of them or work on them. It simply means you should play to your strengths because that will be your identity. Most people do not change their core beliefs and strengths without major focus and work, so let your strengths be the foundation of your leadership.

Your real job is to teach skills, not manage bodies. Managers want to manage tasks and tell their team what to do. True leaders want to coach, take special pride, and show interest in building shadows, but not clones, of themselves. Teaching skills is primarily driven by you finding the strength in others and showing them how to expand their role by leveraging that strength. Good planners should oversee events that require preparation, teachers should oversee training, and outgoing personalities should be in charge of greeting new customers at the door.

The shadows behind you are their own version of themselves but reflect your vision and embody you. As your team grows under this style of leadership, it becomes less and less important for you to be the 'face' of the team and more important to simply listen to their challenges and guide them to better decision-making processes. True leaders lead from behind.

Your innovation as a leader will help harness the skills and talents your team has within them. Once you can do this you go from paving the way for your team to leading them from behind. You watch them pave their own way, which allows you to re-balance your time spent into developing the next set of leaders that will grow in your building. The beauty in all of this is the freedom it allows you. You get to focus on big picture motivations, invest more time in celebrating wins, and give better feedback. The opportunity to observe, coach, and share experiences is one of the most developmental traits that a leader can possess.

Challenge – Complete Your Leadership Shadow

What are your strengths, where are your weaknesses, and what do you need some serious support with?

If you are a chef, finding your lead line cook should be job one. If you write the server schedule, identifying your next server trainer is critical to support your area when you are not around. How complete is your circle of leadership?

What skill set would you like to see in your most trusted team leader? Do the skills you are seeking complement the ones you are bringing to the table, or are you selecting someone because you are similar in style?

Are you wasting time by putting energy into someone because they are like you? Would they enhance your team if they had more responsibility?

KEY GOALS IN THIS CHAPTER

- *Role Players are great, until you need someone to step up and be accountable.*

- *If you start preparing people for their next leadership role, you have in turn made yourself promotable.*

- *Looking across your team, it should be an acceptable loss for any of your team members to leave, because you are setting up every other person to be next-in-line.*

Becoming Unnecessary

There have been times in my life where my work culture revolved around being a role player. People tend to be pigeon-holed into certain roles and this limits their growth. They get so good at one role that they become trapped in it. Now, there is nothing terribly wrong about being a role player, but in my mind, an entire team of role players will probably not find a common mission or achieve great things.

I have heard people jokingly use the expression "Know your role and shut up." Often words are weapons and it scares me to think about what it takes to even offer up that statement. Everyone on a team does have a role to play, but you must also be shown the blueprints to the larger goal of the entire team. It's okay if at first a piece is handed off so that you can play a part in supporting the rest of the team – so long as the goal is that you are mastering a small part in order to be prepared to do a larger role as you go along.

There are some corrosive cultures out there that will stick you into a role and shut down those who attempt to go outside of their boundaries. It may look and sound like everything is on a need-to-know basis, and role players do not need to know anything except their job. The million-dollar question is, what happens when an organization needs these people to be promoted?

I remember being excluded from a meeting of peers that were one step above me and not getting much out of my boss after the meeting. The question I asked myself was, "how can I prepare to be as effective as the other leaders without the same information they receive?" My reflections about my own feelings helped me to figure out what culture I wanted to build in my own leadership team.

I wanted to practice for the role I wanted to be in and be allowed to practice without fear of reprisal. Therefore, I needed to view every leader on my team as if they were getting ready for their next promotion.

This is not to say that some things should not stay confidential. However, I would try my best to not actively withhold the goals, aspirations, and drivers of our business just because of someone's title.

The next week, I scrapped all the red tape levels between the different levels of leadership on my team. I started off with the idea of giving each leader the skills that would be applicable in their next, elevated role. I did my best to prioritize the requests, but also not overwhelm anyone with a slew of new delegation. It was inspiring to see some on my team take on many new skills sets and be able to learn at their own pace over time.

When I challenge my team with something that is new or unknown, it becomes imperative to keep an open door and ask about their comprehension. The process of allowing my leaders to form a question or seek answers is a key of Discovery Leadership. An example is when a new skill is placed on their daily task list - I want to seek them out and gauge their comprehension. If anything is missing that would prevent them from completing their task, I go directly into teaching mode, clarifying the goal and the steps with as much detail as possible. If necessary, I will role model the expectation, or partner them up with a trusted leader. When the task is done, it is equally important to me to follow that conversation up with reflection. What was learned, how did it go, and what could be done differently the next time?

I do not see value in holding back information that can easily be provided to someone who is trying to grow in their role. I feel like I have grown the most under leaders who are open to share, not from those that hold their knowledge close to the vest.

I know that there are tangible fears out there that could prevent you from sharing ideas and goals with your team. There could be a fear of sharing unfinished ideas with others too soon. There is also a fear of becoming overwhelmed and feeling undue pressure to complete work outside of the normal scope. An example is a planned operational change that would require several small transitional steps.

People are not always on board with major changes to the status quo. Think about the complexities of curbside delivery service at a restaurant. If you told all the servers that their job would soon include delivering food to takeout customers in cars outside, the reaction would be predictably negative. However, transitional steps, such as identifying specific servers for to-go service, then creating a separate sale terminal and kiosk, then creating a new job code, and finally delineating a standard operation procedure would be a series of steps that would have a much better reception.

Both perspectives are valid. However, devaluing your team and making them seem as if they are not worthy does absolutely nothing for employee morale, which is a cultural component I hold dear. We need to feed knowledge to our team so they can grow. Even rookie team leaders need a lot of nourishment to grow into the strong leader we want them to be. Withholding information can be crippling to them.

My basic challenge boils down to this – do you think your leaders will need those skills someday? If yes, then you should teach them what you have mastered. If not, think about why you have already written them off. The assumption that they will never be promoted means either a poor hiring decision was made, or you simply gave up on someone's future.

I began to teach everyone on the team the expectations outside of their job code and used cross-training and peer-to-peer coaching to get the knowledge shared. The seismic shift in the team's growth was very close behind. In my first two quarters as a GM, our performance metrics left us below mid-pack in comparison to the rest of the company. After rolling out these new leadership initiatives, we went from last to first in guest satisfaction, and in fact hit the highest guest satisfaction numbers the store had generated. The most impressive part was the longevity - every reporting period after that we were always rated "exceptional" and never "average" again.

My team was high functioning, fully embracing the game plans and were being taught everything they could possibly need to know from trainee all the way up to the GM. When everyone knew and understood their own role, as well as everything they had capacity to understand about the other roles, they covered more territory. I have worked in some big buildings and using zoning assignments to spread out leadership supervision has been a real challenge. Universal leaders with a variety of skill sets make it so much easier to cover all the spaces in-between.

This shift in philosophy allowed us to flourish as a team, but it also prepared everyone for their next role without having to take any steps back in review. This is a world where everything is very fast paced. My team was now prepared for whatever role they needed to play in our growing company. If you needed a GM, Supervisor, Lead Trainer, or Kitchen Manager, we had one waiting and ready to go.

V

Game Plans

KEY GOALS IN THIS CHAPTER

- *By creating a clear set of expectations for every leader, you give them a daily blueprint for personal success.*

- *We will introduce you to a system that will spur a revolution in the communication structure of your team.*

- *This is a radical tool for leaders who want to build a team that will achieve results quickly.*

Starting Out

Early on in my career as a leader of people, I noticed that many things that I simply expected people to get done were slipping through the cracks. Outside of discovering and confronting individuals about singular frustrations, I did not have an answer to this problem right away. A couple of months later, a situation came up that required maximum preparation and execution. In that moment, I stumbled upon a solution that I now hold dear. I would advise any leader going forward to learn and use this tool that I live by day in and day out: daily game plans.

Many team leaders struggle to advance because they have little clue of what to do or what is expected of them daily. Yes, they are professionals and are deserving of a leadership role, but that does not mean they know what they need to do each day. Some self-starters will get certain things accomplished because they are stars in the making. Others will attempt to do things in the building but with little results. This often causes rifts between leaders and their team leaders.

The first thing that many leaders fall back on is "I do not want to micromanage my team," or "I don't have time to micromanage my team." This is fear of setting a tone and has nothing to do with micromanagement. We have already addressed how fear prevents us from acting, and how action steps will ultimately lead to better leadership behaviors.

Leaders think their team is going to come into the building motivated and ready to knock out a punch list of things that they created, observed, or want to own because it means something to them. The reality is the team may just be trying to find their way at work. It is not hard to get lost thinking they are doing a good job, when in your eyes they are not staying on-task or engaging their teams as a leader.

I love these memes that highlight the disparity between what people think their job is versus the expectations that other people have of their role. That is exactly what happens a lot at work. Just because someone has been given a position does not mean they automatically know every function of their role or even what you are expecting them to do. They are not mind readers and often need a nudge from time to time to see what they themselves cannot see.

Nudges are important. I had to get one, and it came unexpectedly from another peer while I was sharing some challenges that I was facing with a new team. This small observation changed the way I started delivering expectations to my team.

"Jeremy you have to micromanage people to get the results you aspire to obtain. Not because they do not already have ability, but you have to help them see what they cannot see."

I took the words to heart. I realized that I had failed at first, because I did the opposite and gave freedom first, too much rope without establishing the basics.

Occasionally, someone will ask me, "do you micromanage?" I find so much negative connotation around this phrase – but today, my answer is "absolutely." I micro-manage the team in terms of development, not as an authoritative figure demanding this and that, but to help them see their development from a common viewpoint.

The first version of my Daily Game Plans was born out of necessity while I was in the games and amusement business. We had a busy holiday season which included a lot of group events that had specific times, activities, and accommodations needed. The prior year some events got sideways due to my lack of delegation and preparation to the team. and I was not going to let that happen again.

The first trial for leaders adopting this method is that game plans take a personal investment of your time up front. It is easier to slide into the false assertion that "my team leaders should just know what they are supposed to do." In a perfect world, sure, but for real people in their true skin, this is not always the case. Selecting good people is just the beginning. Setting them up with realistic goals and expectations daily will establish patterns of behavior. In almost every survey on the topic, consistent performance and job feedback are major contributors to job satisfaction.

I got up early every day to complete the tasks required to open the building and set the stage. I reviewed our daily contracts and grouped the events to make sure everything needed for these events was with the contracts. Then, I delegated the task lists and literally spoon-fed the team every preparation needed to be successful. The results followed soon thereafter, and we had an amazing holiday season with zero issues. My supervisors were pleased with our execution, and the team felt very little stress, both of which made me very proud.

When I went to the theater industry things were totally different. This was not about one or two major events to focus on each day, success meant monitoring dozens of variables through each shift. It felt like there was always something to look at, touch base on, and follow up on. I really needed a tool to keep my team aligned and working towards the same goal. I also needed a way to organize my thoughts and the things I knew as a leader needed to get done. On top of everything else, my team wanted learning opportunities in this tool as well. This resulted in the second version of my daily game plan.

The Game Plan document evolved over time, but what it did was organize my team's actions from the start of the workday to the end of the day. I would assign specific tasks, projects, and development to each person. These tasks had checkboxes next to them so each leader could check off their tasks as they were completed. If a task was not completed, we followed up on our next shift together about the obstacles and solutions. This feedback cycle helped me create moments of micro-development each shift, and for each team member. Discovery Leadership does not always have to be huge awakenings or realizations. The challenges of every day can contribute to developing your team leader's confidence, skill, and efficiency.

At first it was a challenge for me to create detailed game plans every day, but the results spoke for themselves. We had a team that knew exactly what was needed, who was accountable, and kept their focus squarely on progress. The daily game plan was implemented across all departments, and we kept them shared in a common location for all to access.

Systems are born after constant trial and error. When I started seeing real and consistent results, I knew it was time to jot down the rules. I'm positive that no matter what your company does, how many team leaders work for you, or the number of different roles you will manage, game plans will become the singular tool that helps you make every single day a developmental day for your team. Many leaders have read 'One Minute Manager,' and our opinion of this method is that it is OMM on steroids.

KEY GOALS IN THIS CHAPTER

- *Focus on grouping our team based on their skill set and efficiency.*

- *Each person is unique, and your approach to them must change. You can create different success stories by using their individual strengths and goals.*

- *Every day must be focused on becoming more efficient, regardless of hierarchy or tenure.*

- *Each leadership division should be actively pursuing goals that will help them reach the next level.*

The Building Process

Getting a system off the ground is never easy, and this is where your work begins. You may have to get to work 30 minutes early for a while, and if you have a particularly detailed day agenda, it may take an hour of preparation at first. As in most things, what you put into the process determines what you will get out of it; but the passages that follow are a basic explanation of the steps.

I think it is important to remind you that there are vast resources beyond the text on this page. The QR codes at the top of the chapter, or the media references at the end of this book are a gateway to expanded topic discussion, answers to common questions, and direct support from the authors of this system and book.

To begin this process, we will explore the four layers of leadership and some of the common attributes of leaders who fall into each category.

Level 1 – This can be any flavor of 'new' to your team. Common examples might be a newly hired team member, a recently promoted employee, or an employee transferred in from another system. Foundational development is what we are after. The first interval of work experience should focus on task-based expectations only. We are trying to build a routine and explore tasks that have an opportunity for fundamental knowledge growth supported by lots of time for in-depth training. The buzzword here is process mastery – we want new team members to get very good at doing the basic tasks that your business must perform daily in order to operate smoothly.

Ideally, Level 1 leaders are being taught individually and in detail the tasks that are expected of them. Once again, Level 1 game plans should include only tasks, and the number of tasks should be just outside of their capacity. What I mean is that on day one, if their schedule is 9-5, they should still have something left undone at the end of the day, and we utilize our veteran resources to cover up any shortfall. As time goes on, the experience of getting more efficient, prioritization, time management, and skill growth will begin to close that gap. With the right amount of time and coaching, a Level 1 leader should find that all their tasks are easily accomplished within the expected timeframe. A block of their day should look like this:

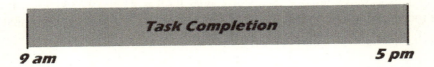

Level 2 – With the structure, self-confidence, and discovery knowledge that your leader builds in Level 1, they should now find some time at the end of each day to begin considering new challenges. My benchmark for successful transition would be 1 hour at the end of each workday to consider future challenges and considerations. A Level 2 leader has the capacity to begin processing their plan of actions for the next day. Their assignments on the daily game plans will include both Tasks and Future Planning.

This is where we begin holding them accountable for setting the next shift up for success or having a close-to-open mindset. As Level 2 leaders progress, there should be a natural shift in their ability to walk into work with a plan, considering that they have already mentally and physically taken steps to begin their tasking routines. As that efficiency creates larger spaces in their day, we begin to introduce ideas of retrospect and looking back at historical situations to form the next level of competence. A Level 2 leader should spend their day like this:

Level 3 – We should have a leader who is very competent and efficient on the day-to-day basics of running the operation. We leverage this skill by asking them to ensure that tasks assigned to all team leaders have reached completion, and they always set the standard for what 'good' looks like. Each shift has zero lag time, because they have arrived at work with a vision for their entire day. This offers an opportunity for them to consider recent results, adapt the methods or strategies, and place communication in front of the right audience to effect change for the better. At Level 3, a leader will be responsible for tasks, future planning, and systems review.

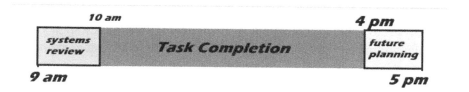

Level 4 – These leaders have continued to set the bar for perfect shift execution. They are timely, punctual, and when they teach, they speak from broad experience and knowledge. A Level 4 manager has been through many challenges and can guide any other team member on the best way to get through any operational situation. Tasks are completed effortlessly and are ingrained so deeply that no reminder or checklist is needed. Although they still spend the same proportion of their day on reviewing results, tasking, and future preparation, their primary goal is to invest a larger percentage of each day into coaching and teaching behaviors. At Level 4, a leader will be assigned tasks, future planning, systems review, and leadership coaching.

These timelines are very generalized but speak to the capacity of each level of experience and the way they allocate their time spent at work. Do not be surprised or scared if you begin with only Level 1 and Level 2 leaders – your job will be to utilize daily game plans that will expand the skills and roles of everyone according to their strengths and drive. One example is new unit openings – where a company will farm in one or two experienced managers, and then 'hire up' a handful of local employees to begin seeding a management team. Your goal is to develop people, no matter what the composition of your team is. Being aware of that team's capacity will make you a successful team leader. Once you have taken the opportunity to assess the individual leaders on your team it becomes time to establish the methodology of creating the Daily Game Plans.

First, think about the tasks that are required to get through the day. They may involve reporting processes, inventories, periodic maintenance checks, or area audits, as well as the things done while opening and closing the business. You may already have a list like this in day-to-day operation, training material, or just on a checklist somewhere. Find the things that you identify as critical, we are going to split those up on the Game Plan.

Below is an example from my business but play along with your own concept requirements and specific task details.

- Red Book Opening Checklist
- Content Programming Check
- Review AM Labor Plan
- AM Safe Count
- AM Shift Floor Management
- Gold Book Walk
- Call Prep Production
- AM Kitchen Line Check

- AM Food Training Presentation
- Mid Shift Sanitation Audit
- AM Staff Times Review
- PM Labor Plan
- Restroom Audit
- PM Shift Floor Management
- PM Kitchen Line Check

- PM Food Training Presentation
- PM Bar & Restaurant Management
- Daily Labor Review
- Red Book Closing Checklist
- PM Safe Count / Deposit
- Verify Voucher Counts

Now, we are going to divide these tasks up based on each leader's in-time and job location. Once again, I am referencing my workspace, but think about how you would divide up a similar list of tasks in a regular day at your company.

Daily Game Plan

For March 16th, 2020

ALL TEAMS
- ☐
- ☐
- ☐

ANGIE (LEVEL 1) OPENER
- ☐ Red Book Opening Checklist
- ☐ Content Programming Check
- ☐ Review AM Labor Plan
- ☐ AM Safe Count
- ☐ AM Shift Floor Management
- ☐
- ☐
- ☐
- ☐

DANIEL – (LEVEL 2) KITCHEN
- ☐ Red Book Opening Checklist
- ☐ Call Prep Production
- ☐ AM Kitchen Line Check
- ☐ AM Food Training Presentation
- ☐ Mid Shift Sanitation Audit
- ☐ Staff Times review
- ☐
- ☐
- ☐
- ☐

JESSIE – (LEVEL 3) MID-SHIFT
- ☐ PM Labor Deployment Plan
- ☐ Restroom Audit
- ☐ PM Shift Floor Management
- ☐ PM Food Training Presentation
- ☐
- ☐
- ☐
- ☐
- ☐

TOMMY – (LEVEL 4) CLOSER
- ☐ PM Bar & Restaurant Management
- ☐ Daily Labor Review
- ☐ Red Book Closing Checklist
- ☐ Count Safe / Deposit
- ☐ Verify Voucher Counts
- ☐
- ☐
- ☐
- ☐
- ☐
- ☐

Second, walk around your operation with an attentive eye. What are some things that are out of place, need organization, deep cleaning, or repair? Make notes on anything that catches your eye and keep an organized list. It is a great personal goal to use the Gemba walk as a personal list of talking points with your team leaders in a non-confrontational, one-on-one conversation throughout the day. It can also help prevent you from putting too many things on your team's agenda. If you do not have the time to personally detail the items on the list, then you've probably expanded beyond the point of having an impact.

- Water on floor in foyer
- Carts left in customer zones
- Menus not wiped down
- Vacuum doorway entrances
- Deck scrub pos floors
- Mop floor in keg cooler
- Clean manager's office
- All silverware wrapped at end of shift

Realize leaders at all levels can do tasks, and the capacity for doing tasks will increase with your level and efficiency. Try to not overwhelm the new guy with all the 'extra,' and be mindful that tasks without the 'why' will not build the vision and preventative behaviors in managers.

Daily Game Plan

For March 16th, 2020

ALL TEAMS
- ☐
- ☐
- ☐
- ☐

ANGIE (LEVEL 1) OPENER
- ☐ Red Book Opening Checklist
- ☐ Content Programming Check
- ☐ Review AM Labor Plan
- ☐ AM Safe Count
- ☐ AM Shift Floor Management
- ☐ Water on Floor in Foyer
- ☐ Carts left in Customer Zones
- ☐
- ☐

DANIEL – (LEVEL 2) KITCHEN
- ☐ Red Book Opening Checklist
- ☐ Call Prep Production
- ☐ AM Kitchen Line Check
- ☐ AM Food Training Presentation
- ☐ Mid Shift Sanitation Audit
- ☐ Staff Times review
- ☐ Menus Need to be Wiped Down
- ☐ Vacuum Entrance Mats
- ☐
- ☐

JESSIE – (LEVEL 3) MID-SHIFT
- ☐ PM Labor Deployment Plan
- ☐ Restroom Audit
- ☐ PM Shift Floor Management
- ☐ PM Food Training Presentation
- ☐ Deck Scrub POS Floors
- ☐ Mop Floors in Keg Cooler
- ☐
- ☐
- ☐

TOMMY – (LEVEL 4) CLOSER
- ☐ PM Bar & Restaurant Management
- ☐ Daily Labor Review
- ☐ Red Book Closing Checklist
- ☐ Count Safe / Deposit
- ☐ Verify Voucher Counts
- ☐ Clean Manager's Office
- ☐
- ☐
- ☐
- ☐
- ☐

Third, look over the team calendar, event binder, and company-wide messages to help prepare the team for upcoming events for the day. The goal is to see what needs to be done, whether it is a team meeting, company-wide event, pricing change, or new protocols. We want to be in control of the day and not let the day control or catch us off guard. Being proactive and not reactive is the key to every team's success and it starts with a game plan that addresses the five Ps: proper preparation prevents poor performance.

- Banquet Event at 5:30 PM – SysCorp Group, 50 people, buffet and meeting in Events Room

- Featured Content night – Special Screening of 'Teen Wolf' in Theater 3 at 7:30 pm

Daily Game Plan

For March 16th, 2020

ALL TEAMS
- ☐
- ☐
- ☐
- ☐

ANGIE (LEVEL 1) OPENER
- ☐ Red Book Opening Checklist
- ☐ Content Programming Check
- ☐ Review AM Labor Plan
- ☐ AM Safe Count
- ☐ AM Shift Floor Management
- ☐ Water on Floor in Foyer
- ☐ Carts left in Customer Zones
- ☐
- ☐

DANIEL – (LEVEL 2) KITCHEN
- ☐ Red Book Opening Checklist
- ☐ Call Prep Production
- ☐ AM Kitchen Line Check
- ☐ AM Food Training Presentation
- ☐ Mid Shift Sanitation Audit
- ☐ Staff Times review
- ☐ Menus Need to be Wiped Down
- ☐ Vacuum Entrance Mats
- ☐ Banquet Prep – Use Checklist
- ☐

JESSIE – (LEVEL 3) MID-SHIFT
- ☐ PM Labor Deployment Plan
- ☐ Restroom Audit
- ☐ PM Shift Floor Management
- ☐ PM Food Training Presentation
- ☐ Deck Scrub POS Floors
- ☐ Mop Floors in Keg Cooler
- ☐ Banquet Food Prepared
- ☐
- ☐

TOMMY – (LEVEL 4) CLOSER
- ☐ PM Bar & Restaurant Management
- ☐ Daily Labor Review
- ☐ Red Book Closing Checklist
- ☐ Count Safe / Deposit
- ☐ Verify Voucher Counts
- ☐ Clean Manager's Office
- ☐ 'Teen Wolf' Screening Prep
- ☐ Greet Banquet Guests
- ☐
- ☐
- ☐

Forward-looking activities should be delegated to your level 2, 3, and 4 managers. Basically, we want the new folks to continue to focus on tasking efficiency and make sure we are building the vision of level 2 managers.

Fourth, review your communication platforms emails, message boards, slack, or communication logs to observe what notes the team left about the previous shift. Take note of any key items that were discussed to help navigate the team and keep them aware of the issues that took place the day before. Your level 3 & 4 managers are primarily responsible for systems review, as they should have wisdom from having made decisions and seeing the results over time. Partnering up these managers with Level 1 & 2 folks is a great way to help build their teaching & coaching skills and add experience and perspective to the 1 & 2s.

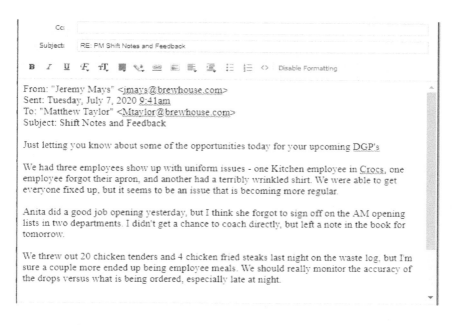

Your level 3 & 4 managers are primarily responsible for systems review, as they should have wisdom from having made decisions and seeing the results over time. Partnering up these managers with Level 1 & 2 folks is a great way to help build their teaching and coaching skills and add experience and perspective to the 1 & 2s.

Daily Game Plan

For March 16th, 2020

ALL TEAMS
- ☐
- ☐
- ☐

ANGIE (LEVEL 1) OPENER
- ☐ Red Book Opening Checklist
- ☐ Content Programming Check
- ☐ Review AM Labor Plan
- ☐ AM Safe Count
- ☐ AM Shift Floor Management
- ☐ Water on Floor in Foyer
- ☐ Carts left in Customer Zones
- ☐
- ☐

DANIEL – (LEVEL 2) KITCHEN
- ☐ Red Book Opening Checklist
- ☐ Call Prep Production
- ☐ AM Kitchen Line Check
- ☐ AM Food Training Presentation
- ☐ Mid Shift Sanitation Audit
- ☐ Staff Times review
- ☐ Menus Need to be Wiped Down
- ☐ Vacuum Entrance Mats
- ☐ Banquet Prep – Use Checklist
- ☐

JESSIE – (LEVEL 3) MID-SHIFT
- ☐ PM Labor Deployment Plan
- ☐ Restroom Audit
- ☐ PM Shift Floor Management
- ☐ PM Food Training Presentation
- ☐ Deck Scrub POS Floors
- ☐ Mop Floors in Keg Cooler
- ☐ Banquet Food Prepared
- ☐ Validate Department Books, respond with feedback to Dept. openers and Managers
- ☐

TOMMY – (LEVEL 4) CLOSER
- ☐ PM Bar & Restaurant Management
- ☐ Daily Labor Review
- ☐ Red Book Closing Checklist
- ☐ Count Safe / Deposit
- ☐ Verify Voucher Counts
- ☐ Clean Manager's Office
- ☐ 'Teen Wolf' Screening Prep
- ☐ Greet Banquet Guests
- ☐ Ensure 100% Completion on Department Books at close
- ☐ Schedule Performance Review for team members with recurring uniform issues
- ☐

Finally, we want to extract the information from two tools we have utilized -- one on one conversations and leadership observations -- to add some variance in each person's game plan. The real question is, how do you move each person to the next level?

    Level 1 should have a forward-looking goal
    Level 2 should have a goal to review past performance
    Level 3 should have a coaching challenge
    Level 4 should have a leadership vision challenge

Think about how you are going to advance the leadership development of each of your team leaders. Of all the items on the DGP, this entry has the lowest cost and the highest reward. Simply identifying that there is a goal will encourage your team leaders to invest in a shared success story.

Daily Game Plan

For March 16th, 2020

ALL TEAMS
- ☐
- ☐
- ☐
- ☐

ANGIE (LEVEL 1) OPENER
- ☐ Red Book Opening Checklist
- ☐ Content Programming Check
- ☐ Review AM Labor Plan
- ☐ AM Safe Count
- ☐ AM Shift Floor Management
- ☐ Water on Floor in Foyer
- ☐ Carts left in Customer Zones
- ☐ Set a personal reminder to yourself about checking uniforms tomorrow
- ☐

DANIEL – (LEVEL 2) KITCHEN
- ☐ Red Book Opening Checklist
- ☐ Call Prep Production
- ☐ AM Kitchen Line Check
- ☐ AM Food Training Presentation
- ☐ Mid Shift Sanitation Audit
- ☐ Staff Times review
- ☐ Menus Need to be Wiped Down
- ☐ Vacuum Entrance Mats
- ☐ Banquet Prep - Use Checklist
- ☐ Review last night's closing waste log and identify three items to reduce waste tonight

JESSIE – (LEVEL 3) MID-SHIFT
- ☐ PM Labor Deployment Plan
- ☐ Restroom Audit
- ☐ PM Shift Floor Management
- ☐ PM Food Training Presentation
- ☐ Deck Scrub POS Floors
- ☐ Mop Floors in Keg Cooler
- ☐ Banquet Food Prepared
- ☐ Validate Department Books, respond with feedback to Dept. openers and Managers
- ☐ Validate Angie's opening | side-by-side and share ideas of how openers can prepare for Banquet Events

TOMMY – (LEVEL 4) CLOSER
- ☐ PM Bar & Restaurant Management
- ☐ Daily Labor Review
- ☐ Red Book Closing Checklist
- ☐ Count Safe / Deposit
- ☐ Verify Voucher Counts
- ☐ Clean Manager's Office
- ☐ 'Teen Wolf' Screening Prep
- ☐ Greet Banquet Guests
- ☐ Ensure 100% Completion on Department Books at close
- ☐ Schedule Performance Review for team members with recurring uniform issues
- ☐ Audit Banquet 'Best Practices' to see if we performed well, or if there are recommends for improvement

In the common theme section, identify some items on your list that all team leaders are expected to accomplish. Perhaps it is auditing sales tickets or inspecting restrooms for cleanliness. Additionally, you can add lessons learned from recent trends in the business, sales goals, weather, or anything you want to share or task across all team leaders.

Finally, do you have developmental goals for your team leaders? If not, it is a best practice to make goal setting a regular part of each leader's week. Today is always a great time to schedule a sit down with a team leader in the very near future. In this way, we offer each person a clear picture of the day's requirements and expectations. We design a schedule that matches their skill set and present capacity. We also offer them challenges and developmental thought processes that will prepare them for the next level. These examples are merely for reference and for helping you begin the process of writing game plans. In the real world, your leaders may have many entries for their stretch goals, more or less tasks, and different scheduled tasks. The one thing that will encourage the most growth is to seek feedback on their goal progress and daily challenges. Guiding your team leaders to reflect on their experiences is a core tenet of Discovery Leadership, even if it is just a line or two about their successes or failures that day.

Daily Game Plan

For March 16th, 2020

ALL TEAMS
- [ ] End of Shift Communication
- [ ] Stay in zones as much as possible
- [ ] Audit Uniform Compliance
- [ ] All Departments complete their Daily Checklists

ANGIE (LEVEL 1) OPENER
- [ ] Red Book Opening Checklist
- [ ] Content Programming Check
- [ ] Review AM Labor Plan
- [ ] AM Safe Count
- [ ] AM Shift Floor Management
- [ ] Water on Floor in Foyer
- [ ] Carts left in Customer Zones
- [ ] Set a personal reminder to yourself about checking uniforms tomorrow
- [ ] Review Weekly Goal Progress Week 4 with me today at 4:00

DANIEL – (LEVEL 2) KITCHEN
- [ ] Red Book Opening Checklist
- [ ] Call Prep Production
- [ ] AM Kitchen Line Check
- [ ] AM Food Training Presentation
- [ ] Mid Shift Sanitation Audit
- [ ] Staff Times review
- [ ] Menus Need to be Wiped Down
- [ ] Vacuum Entrance Mats
- [ ] Banquet Prep – Use Checklist
- [ ] Review last night's closing waste log and identify three items to reduce waste tonight

JESSIE – (LEVEL 3) MID-SHIFT
- [ ] PM Labor Deployment Plan
- [ ] Restroom Audit
- [ ] PM Shift Floor Management
- [ ] PM Food Training Presentation
- [ ] Deck Scrub POS Floors
- [ ] Mop Floors in Keg Cooler
- [ ] Banquet Food Prepared
- [ ] Validate Department Books, respond with feedback to Dept. openers and Managers
- [ ] Validate Angie's opening side-by-side and share ideas of how openers can prepare for Banquet Events

TOMMY – (LEVEL 4) CLOSER
- [ ] PM Bar & Restaurant Management
- [ ] Daily Labor Review
- [ ] Red Book Closing Checklist
- [ ] Count Safe / Deposit
- [ ] Verify Voucher Counts
- [ ] Clean Manager's Office
- [ ] 'Teen Wolf' Screening Prep
- [ ] Greet Banquet Guests
- [ ] Ensure 100% Completion on Department Books at close
- [ ] Schedule Performance Review for team members with recurring uniform issues
- [ ] Audit Banquet 'Best Practices' to see if we performed well, or if there are recommends for improvement

Your job as a coach is to recognize each level, each person's space, and be available for support and development. Level 1 folks are going to need tons of immediate praise, detailed instructions, and dedicated time for feedback about how their day went. Level 4 folks are going to need structured time to really help them analyze the results of their leadership challenges, and continuous pressure to establish role-model behaviors in all their tasks.

The cheerleader role is equally important. Establishing a culture of praise looks different to folks in each level. Your senior leaders do not necessarily want to be praised for completing a menial task that they have done to perfection hundreds of times, but a Level 1 leader may seek positive praise for even the smallest task completed. Praise for a Level 4 leader may be inviting them to lead the next team meeting, rolling out a new operational platform, or spearheading an improvement task force – all of which could be excruciatingly stressful or humiliating to a new manager.

For those of you who like immediate gratification, you will be able to track your progress by watching your maintenance list get smaller and smaller each day, and your team leaders engaging in their goals on a daily basis.

In the long term, you will see your team leaders begin to participate in self-assignment of tasks, increased efficiency, better communication, and goal accomplishment. Here lies the true recipe of building a high performing team that is a custom fit to each person's unique skill set.

Quick Recap – Building Game Plans

1. Assess your leadership team, grouping them by skill. This determines the complexity of tasks that you will assign them.

2. Identify the core tasks that must be done every single day. Divide them across the group, depending on the leader's skill level, in-time, department, or permissions set.

3. Use a Gemba walk to identify coachable opportunities for change. Add these to the appropriate levels and plan to coach the 'why'.

4. Look for opportunities to get ahead, through prep or planning. Assign these tasks to the appropriate levels.

5. Challenge those in a veteran leadership role to analyze team performance, and to share those results with junior leaders.

6. Challenge all levels of leaders to try a skill just outside of their competence or comfort zone.

7. Set basic reminders for all team members.

8. Try to budget some time for one-on-one goal setting with a team leader every workday.

KEY GOALS IN THIS CHAPTER

- *Over time, using a plan develops behaviors that will increase efficiency and team growth.*

- *Your ability to challenge leaders in their daily goals will dictate the speed of their development.*

- *Adding one-on-one time to reflect on the lessons learned from daily game plans is an easy way to begin a conversation.*

Expanding Roles

The biggest outcome from establishing Daily Game Plans is setting new patterns of behavior. Think about a time where you had a series of tasks to do but had not experienced them all yet. Perhaps this looks like an office opening task list, or an inventory analysis, or even a facilities checklist.

On your first time doing the list, it may take you hours. Doing things daily, you become more fluid in your lists, your detail becomes more specific, and your task gets completed in less time. The use of Daily Game Plans helped my team leaders to simply knock out more and more task-based skills every day. This opened more of their day to coaching, personal development, or simply advancing the overall quality of our operation.

As an example, my kitchen manager had a daily and weekly game plan he created for his supervisors. This gave them a system to follow that guaranteed that they could double check prep lists, pull product to thaw, complete department line checks, and so on. This game plan was a simple idea but powerful. It gave them structure so that they could build a routine. Each new day's Game Plan allowed me to then add projects within their daily tasks. As they became accustomed to doing everyday tasks on schedule as well as dive into improved operation, I began to fold in single items that focused on their personal leadership development.

This structure is no different than your teacher having a daily routine when you walk into their classroom. You have an outline of things to do, but you complete things in your own way, you add value in your own way, and you utilize your style in your own way.

Take a trip down memory lane and think back to which teacher's class you did the best in. Most people get excited thinking about the nicest teacher that gave them a good grade or that class that you had all your friends in, but if you dig into it, we can probably agree that the most demanding and structured teachers brought out the best in you.

I think about a teacher who was strict, prepared, organized, and had a routine game plan ready for our class every day. There was no hanging out and talking. I was simply trying to ensure that I kept up and passed that class, because that teacher was all business. Every day our class came in and knew the routine. The tasks and projects led to real comprehension and development, and, not surprisingly, I became much more efficient and knowledgeable in that subject and I still think of that experience as a very positive one in my life.

The same thing applies to the daily game plans. I want to build out for my team a structured approach that challenges them every day. Everyone saw what was on each other's game plans, so it was easy for anyone on the team to follow up on completion or know when to offer a helping hand. No one wanted to be the one who could not get their list done because everyone knew it was built exactly to their strengths and capacity.

These game plans are detailed but allowed for individuality and growth. As you grow in your role as part of my team, the more freedom and flexibility you have in your game plan. However, you had to earn your way to that level of trust. If you remember back to my own life lessons, freedom to try new ideas is a great developmental tool but starting with a mastery-level set of skills as your foundation is what will help to make real strides.

Even my leaders-in-training have game plans, regardless if they are staying in my system or transferring to another unit after their training process. I want them to be a part of the team immediately, but I also wanted them to get in the habit of following the routine we did in our location. Nobody on my leadership team is excluded from game plans, including myself. I am always eager to do my part so the team can see we are all on the same team. I try to set the standard of what I expect out of their role in the same tasks.

Yes, this leadership development tool took time, but nothing great ever came for free, and Rome was not built in a day. Have you ever had to sit down with a supervisor and explain why things that were due days or weeks ago had not been completed? It is so simple for small tasks to fall by the wayside, especially if there is not a daily feedback loop to support their progress.

This simple tool allowed me to guide my team without having to always spend 15-30 minutes asking if this was done or that was done or wondering who is going to own a task. I knew who was in charge and I could walk by and look at something on the game plan that I created previously and know whether it was done or not. Yes, I invested time up front, but I was able to get all that time and more on the back end. It was so much more fulfilling to spend time early in the morning to write up our blueprint for success, rather than needing to stick around late every night chasing deadlines and still feeling like nothing had been accomplished.

Have you ever worked in a job where you felt like you were always busy, but never getting ahead? It is such an easy trap to get caught in a task, without planning, delegating, and following up. There are a million books written about all these topics, but I cannot help but think the only thing that was really needed was a good Daily Game Plan.

Game Plans can become great as status symbols as well, without being discriminatory or biased. If you were a senior manager, you probably have big cultural ideas that need to be attacked and spend less time on task management. I need these proven performers to use those built-up leadership skills to make real decisions.

The final nuance is that I also dedicate personal time for each team member at a minimum of once every two weeks. They get an advance email and calendar reminder, and then I place that item on their game plan so they could prepare in advance for our conversation.

If you have never conducted a one-on-one meeting or have difficulty setting out conversation points, previous game plans will become invaluable. It allows both of you to simply review the tasks done, opportunities communicated, and missed goals from the previous shifts. This in turn will place you squarely in the driver's seat to challenge leaders to set goals for themselves without much prodding.

Leaders will invariably find tasks or challenges that they cannot complete satisfactorily. A basic lesson in Root Cause analysis is that struggles can be identified as coming from lack of planning, communication, or effort. You can solve, together, for the true reason why a challenge cannot be surpassed. We have already talked about the negative impact of simply laying down more tasks or nit-picking details that do not shape leadership behaviors. Addressing that root cause and guiding your team to suggest solutions will inspire your team to believe in your vision as a leader. You will become the one they trust to be a guide on their path to discover their own solutions. Here is a real-world example of a great Daily Game Plan from my kitchen leadership team:

Daily Game Plans

OPENER
- (7:00am- 8:00 am) Open the Building
- Assess Back Dock Cleanliness
- Print Sheets needed for the Day:
  a. Bulk Prep
  b. Cool Down Log
  c. Waste Log
  d. Roster
  e. Daily Plan
  f. Labor Card
  g. Pre-shift sheet
- Call Prep
- **Validate Yesterday's Cool Down Log**
- Log On KDS
- Turn on Equipment; Ovens, Flat Top, Pizza Oven
- Check cooler temps
- Make notes on close
- Check in staff
- Check Admits times and numbers (write on labor card)
- Do orders if applicable
- Pre-shift with Staff
- (10:00 am-12:00 pm) Line Check
- Drive lunch
- Validate Prep (productivity, accuracy, **cool down, quality**)
- Organize coolers
- Do any orders by cut-off time
- Assess labor, check out staff, make outs
- (1:00 pm-3:00 pm) Gold Book tasks, 3 hours temps, do any corrective action needed.
- Enter Prep from previous day in COMPEAT
- Organize coolers
- **Slack Thaw Proteins**
- Invoices, Prep Calls, Waste log entered
- Validate clock-in/clock out times for TMs (KM/AKM)

MID
- Do pre-shift with closer (discuss any closing issues from previous night)
- (10:00am- 1pm) Check in with Opener
  a. Prep 911s
  b. Staff Issues
  c. Equipment Issues
  d. Set-Up the Plan
- Validate Prep (productivity, accuracy, **cool down log, quality**)
- Main Kitchen Focus: Expo, Ticket times, Food Quality
- Validate Line Prep (productivity, accuracy, **cool down log**)
- (1:00 pm-3 pm) Assist with Gold Book Tasks: 3 hr. Temp, Dish Log, Mid-Day Sanitation Audit
- Assist with Cooler organization
- Update Admits on Labor cards
- Let Openers and closers make cuts (use radio to help communicate who is ready)
- Assist with Invoices and prep call into COMPEAT if needed
- Drive PM Prime Set: Tickets, Food Quality, Expo
- Cooler Organization
- Validate Slack Thaw of Proteins
- (7:00 pm-9:00 pm) Validate PM prep and Cool Downs
- Check out with Closer

CLOSER
- (3:00 pm-5:00 pm) Pre-Shift with Opener
- Review Gold Book for any missed tasks
- Check in PM staff
- Position your Roster
- (4:00 pm-6:00 pm) Line Check
- Pre-Shift with staff
- Set up plan with Mid Supervisor
- (5:00 pm-9:00 pm) Prime Set
- 1st cut start to clean
- Make cuts
- Organize coolers
- Validate Slack Thaw of Proteins
- **Validate Cool down complete for the day** (initials on log)
- Produce Order
- (10:30am – 12:00 am) Use closing checklist to check staff (Gold Book) **(Station Kits are 100%)**
- Enter Waste Log into COMPEAT
- **Validate clean pans and fully stocked after flipping.**
- Drains- validate all drains are clean/dry/treated
- Dish- follow "dish closing guidelines"
- Fans- 1 down in dish room & 2 down in prep (positioned to flow over drains)

GET TO THE "ROOT" OF THE PROBLEM

Staffing- Call outs, NCNS, Late, Rostered wrong, In-time wrong, negativity, uniform standard, sending someone home (is it the right thing to do?)

Routine- Gold Book tasks (Line Check, Dish Log, cool down, PPP, & Mid-day sanitation audit), Ordering/Receiving, Calling Prep, Service execution, closing checklist, & **The Daily Plan**

Communication- Product issues (Prep 911s), Staff issues, Equipment issues, re-cap the shift, coaching the staff (feedback), write notes, & Set-up the plan (pow wow at the prep table)

Same Language The Daily Plan

SHIFT CHANGE FOCUS
- Trash and boxes are thrown out
- Slicer is cleaned
- Top stock done (each station)
- Floors swept
- Tables wiped down

AM is checking out with Opener

KEY GOALS IN THIS CHAPTER

- *Knowing how to transition from tasks to leadership starts with transitioning team members from doing a task to contributing to a system.*

- *Mastering any system takes practice, patience, and time. However, once elevated a leader can use the system instead of just being a part of it.*

Tasking to Leading

You will find that there are incredibly rewarding results of continuing to drive Daily Game Plans for your team. Let me tell you about Anita, who started her journey on our leadership team as an entry-level supervisor. I knew her core values offered the potential to create a very powerful leader in a short amount of time. I knew I needed to push the boundaries of what she thought was possible, and her path has been inspiring.

As she moved through the process, Anita's task-based game plans quickly grew as her capacity increased. I trusted her more and more each day, and the quality of her work was always on-point. She would look at her game plan, see 10-15 items, notice the light load on others and then shake her head in silence. She was furious, and I knew it, but her capacity was far greater than those around her. This meant to pull the greatness out of her, I had to push harder and further outside her comfort zone. She dominated and owned everything on the list. If she could not get to it, she gave me a detailed text, email, or phone call. It was almost as if in spite, to say, "Why should I have to do so much more than my peers?"

Flash forward six months later, and she was invited to a leadership summit with many of her peers from other locations that all had one common goal of becoming General Managers. When she entered the room, she was nervous and unsure if she was ready to be in the same room with these other aspiring leaders. The whole group was locked in the same room for four days, discussing strategy, their daily routines, and how they were advancing the agenda of the company and themselves. Hearing the words and perspectives of her peers, Anita realized that she had become more of a leader than she thought.

In this moment of discovery, she faced a fear of failing in front of peers because she felt they were more advanced than her based on tenure in their roles. However, what began showing through her was knowledge, innovation, and most importantly, her confidence. As they walked through lesson after lesson, she discovered the game plans she once rolled her eyes at had given her a foundation that the others did not have. In those moments of discovery, she realized her capacity had grown beyond those she was sitting next to, because her game plans had challenged her, developed her, enhanced her to a level not even she was aware of.

Her daily routine, based on months of knowing exactly what was expected of her through Game Plan design, was far more robust than even the most veteran manager in her peer group The tool that she used to communicate common goals and expectations to the other leaders on her team were miles ahead of what the others were using for accountability. While the peer group had minimal systems to build upon, she had built a foundation that groomed her based on her individual strengths.

The structure of the game plans had allowed her to cross off leadership tasks without even noticing. She was being groomed to be an elite leader – not an average leader. It was now apparent how productive she had become because of all the discovery learning she had done. This allowed her to teach what she was taught – even in a group setting where she thought she was underdeveloped. It was a moment where Anita realized she was ready to lead lions.

I left that conference to catch a flight to a new store opening, and I got a call from Anita.

"Thank you for pushing me so hard. I knew you were giving me more attention and challenges than the others, but after seeing so many people who wish they could have the skill set that I have, I now understand the "Why" behind what you do."

That is a moment that every leader should get to feel, and this is exactly the type of growth we should all see from those in our shadow.

While I was away, I needed someone to take up my responsibility of giving the team leaders their Daily Game Plans, and Anita was a natural choice. As the others grew and would get their 10-15 tasks that she created, she would giggle and simply say "I know, I know. I have been down that road, and you will soon understand why I am asking these things from you." She had discovered the energy it took to be successful and was now applying this lesson to the team members below her.

Anita was completing the cycle. She was now the craftswoman working on becoming a master by teaching it to the team. She was able to be the leader of the building because she now had the foresight to see what each day entailed, how to support the team in their struggles, and how to handle the curve balls of the day to day because she had already discovered her way to leadership.

A key point to make here is that Anita's title and pay did not change, but her influence and leadership meant she was ready for whatever challenge was ahead of her. I told her months before she arrived at this beautiful moment that she did not need a title to be a leader. Now, here she was discovering that very statement was true.

KEY GOALS IN THIS CHAPTER

- *A system is stronger than just having strong individual members.*

- *Looking for opportunities to build a team with complementary strengths will increase the probability of achieving team goals.*

- *Game Plans can be the foundation of your operation. As teams grow the checklist will reflect team improvements and not tasks.*

- *"Great" only happens when you build a system that will support other people discovering, earning scars, and challenging their boundaries.*

Systems Build Satisfaction

Picture the Pyramids in Egypt. What image comes into your mind at first? Here is my guess:

But here is the thing – there are about 80 pyramids in some state of existence, but we mostly think about those three giant feats of engineering, or maybe only the Great Pyramid built for Khufu. Although we are talking about 1,000 years of cultural and engineering development, the Pyramids allow us to see how a system can slowly grow, improve, and get better over time. Each successive Pharaoh who wanted a bigger and better structure would have had to build on the knowledge, successes, and methodology of everything that had come before to take it to the next step.

Think about the organization of teams in that scenario – thousands of quarry workers, farmers, engineers, masons, painters, and even interior decorators were needed. All these teams had to work in tandem, in a terribly hot environment, and over decades to accomplish their goal. Each team had to find leadership that would be knowledgeable of the past, but also look to innovate in their current role. It took a natural growth over the millennia to reach that level of organizational structure.

However, their dedication and craftsmanship has stood the test of time. You have got to know they were open to creative thought as well – how the heck else did the Sphinx get past the building committee?

Flash forward 3,600 years to a team meeting in my tiny world. We were wrapping up a team meeting by sharing our success stories from the previous weekend. My kitchen manager offered up that our greatest strength was our ability to adapt, and I could not have agreed more.

We adapted by making key notes of things that occurred during the day that affected us, and we planned for ways to get ahead of those same issues in the next day. Maybe it was adding staff in a critical location, ramping up production of a featured item, or dedicating a shift leader into a role during a bottleneck situation. Whatever the case was, we were able to take note of it and put it on the next day's game plan to make sure we put our energy into the right place, and at the right times.

This was irrefutable evidence for me that my team had developed three behaviors that I hold dear. First, they were willing to identify their opportunities – struggles or challenges – that they knew could be better. Second, they were willing to communicate with each other to develop a better path, a solution, and put it in writing. Third, they were not afraid of taking steps and making decisions that would impact the business, because they knew that acting was a natural part of growth and "proactive not reactive" was our motto.

Having the game plans as a system gave the entire team a platform to share their ideas and ultimately make life better for everyone in the building. Our execution relied on the foundations built around that process.

I am happy to admit that there are some people who can do amazing things all by themselves. I also would assert that it is extremely difficult to build a team dynamic around a mindset that refuses to be helped or keep up with the group. I know a lot of great of architects that have amazing blueprints, but you still need a team to get a skyscraper off the ground.

Systems allow you to magnify, interlock, and develop different people in different ways. You get to use the whole team as a giant pool of different skill sets and behaviors. Baseball's Joe DiMaggio might have been one of the greatest hitters and fielders of all-time but did you ever see that guy pitch a game? Think of your team leaders as position players, and Daily Game Plans as a puzzle. Your job is to put each person into the space with their greatest strengths, support them with others who complement their weaknesses, and give them a plan that pushes them to grow in their own space.

Envision a day where you can walk into your building and be there for hours without anyone needing you because they have their daily game plan in their hand executing your vision and living their blueprints to perfection. The game plan allows you to be there for key moments, to show up and test your team, have important coaching conversations, and have honest moments of reflection about their decision making process at the time that they are making those choices.

I speak to my team leaders about my idea of a perfect shift in my role as a GM. I would come in, grab a cup of coffee, walk the building to validate systems in place, and then sit down at a table without the pressure of having to put out fires or 'fix' anything. At the point where game plans were in full effect, I saw the ownership and accountability rise and surpass my expectations. It took a lot of work, but when things went from talk to reality for me, I could not have been more satisfied in my job and proud of my team.

The beautiful part that is often missed is the camaraderie that comes with this. Teams must work together because their game plans are intertwined. Each person is a fundamental component of a machine. Doing your own part is just as important as making sure the next person can do theirs as well. Without fail the team communicates and supports each other because the end goal is the same for every person on the team.

Your Daily Game Plans will soon become a living document – they should continuously adapt to the priorities of your workspace, be available for all to contribute, and be something your team looks forward to because of the inherent value they offer.

VI

Inspired Team Meetings

KEY GOALS IN THIS CHAPTER

- *Deliver a meeting that is focused on audience participation and you observing their interactions*
- *Plan your meetings so that people have an opportunity to prepare and present their ideas*
- *Focus on behaviors and development, not task lists or calendars*
- *Ask questions that will challenge the status quo*
- *Use common discussion to arrive at the true goals of the team*

Progressive Meetings

The words 'Manager Meeting' used to send a small shiver down my spine. Styrofoam coffee cups, stale muffins, and plastic tables seem to be all I could remember of manager meetings, until a very changing experience showed up in my world. On a high level, I knew what I wanted out of manager meetings – engagement, participation, a sense of purpose, and getting the team aligned. This is the story of how I learned to forget everything I knew about meetings. To walk away from dictatorial, task driven communication and venture into the realm of inclusivity, development, and progress was a watershed moment for our team.

At this meeting Matthew, one of my veteran leaders and the co-author of this book asked to lead a small section of my meeting, which was fine by me. After a short introduction to the topic, he began by asking each of the team leaders challenging questions about their role in the topics, and the team struggled to answer.

I watched as the dynamic of the meeting changed in an instant. The team became alert, aware, and engaged because they had been put on the spot. Matthew was working as my lawyer, cross-examining each team leader in the room and making them think about the answers they gave. They sharpened their responses, made eye contact, and he elevated the entire room in that moment.

I cherish the Discovery moments when I can see that I was wrong. On this day I was shown that I had been failing my team with each meeting. Like previous leaders I had learned how to run a 'traditional' meeting. They began with me giving the team an agenda of my talking points and ended with a few tasks for them to speak on. In my meetings, my team listened and took notes, but mostly worked on staying awake.

They were not engaged or part of the conversation. These meetings had provided them with zero opportunity to participate or develop.

I was forced to be an observer at that point. I saw the leader of the meeting prioritize engagement, and I saw the reaction of the listeners. If you have ever been on-stage, like in a talent show or karaoke, you can understand how difficult it is to really *see* your audience. Those bright lights and the pressure of the moment can completely blind you to your own impact. I found out that by passing the mic, I could look on and really assess my method. I immediately made plans to do things differently.

After the meeting, we went into the office and I could not speak fast enough, telling Matthew I must change my entire meeting structure. Confused, he asked me what I meant by that. I stated, "I have failed the team up until this point. You used your time as the speaker to build energy, and then put them in a Discovery mindset. I watched you challenge them in ways I have not, and I saw the team's response in a new way." I changed my entire meeting style that day and in that moment.

I asked myself those questions and answered them to Matthew. We worked on an agenda that transformed years of complacency into the talk of our organization. These meetings inspired leaders and helped cultivate a culture of collaboration. Let me share our new process with you.

> Think about your last meeting.
>
> How did it go?
> What do you remember?
> What was your role?
> What did you learn?
> What captivated you?
> Did you leave inspired?

First things first, I had to set the date. No one likes surprises, and if you are setting an expectation that people should be prepared, then the time and location should be known well in advance. It also eliminates that excuse of "I didn't know..." right out of the gates. I put it on the calendar, sent an email reminder with date and time, and I even added preparation time to the daily game plans.

Next, I needed a big idea. This takes a little soul searching, and input from trusted voices on my team. I like inviting one or two of my senior leaders for a chat over lunch. I start with a series of questions to spur on conversation.

- What is our biggest leadership opportunity right now?
- What challenges can we not get past?
- What opportunities keep us from being great, right now?
- Is there something coming up we need to address as an entire team?

These thoughts birth the main topics of the meeting agenda – but I also want to keep it tight on time. A meeting that lasts more than an hour is taxing, and it is hard to cover more than three real topics in-depth with that constraint. For example, if we identify "communication" as a primary opportunity I want to set an expectation of what good communication looks like, challenge the leaders to address their personal standards of communication, and get a commitment to change for the better.

With those three goals in mind, next I look for inspiration. This is usually as simple as a YouTube video or a passage from an influential book. From this point, I can launch into a personal expression of what good "looks like." I need to paint the picture for my audience, show them what an ideal version of communication is in my mind. This is my voice, and it needs to be in words that will show my dedication to improving the situation.

Then, I look for an engaging question that will stimulate my fellow team leaders to really think about their role. This step requires you to have already done the Discovery process with those you will challenge. If you have a lot of managers, do not feel like you must do this step for every single name tag in the room. Pick people that have an opportunity to inspire, or leaders who may be considered the weakest link in the communication chain.

For example, let us say Suzy is leaving great feedback on shift operations, and Dan is merely checking the boxes. My planned line of questioning would be different for Dan than it would be for Suzy. The ultimate goal is to bring everyone to common ground.

Dan, what benefit do you think shift communication has on our team? What is the minimum amount of communication you would expect to see from a team member?

At this point I have challenged Dan to raise his personal standards, but also to do it in a public forum. There are very few motivators more effective than the fear of being a hypocrite, and I would allow the speech to help drive the action. My plan would be to then turn to Suzy.

Suzy, can you think of a time where communication you received helped you to avoid an obstacle or save the day? What would have happened if you had been blind to that situation?

For Suzy, we are giving her a voice to be passionate and reinforce the true value of a behavior. This immediately elevates the average standard for all who are listening. It starts to sell your other leaders on the 'why' behind the task.

There are many books about how to 'identify the gap' between expected behavior and actual behavior. However, when people speak in their own words it is easier to see what needs to happen. Mind you, this is not to shame or call out anyone. If you are truly going to build a team of strength, we must also have the courage to confront the things that make us different and understand compromise.

I end by asking for commitments from the group at large. There is no person in charge of answering – this should be a round-table discussion, but the group will quickly find "the center" of the argument and come together. In the above scenario, perhaps the group decides that the closing manager should add a note of recommendation to the opening manager, by adding a specific entry on the Daily Game Plan for the next day.

Regardless of where the center ends up being, it is your job to make sure that the common goals of the entire team have advanced beyond the space they were in when the team walked into the meeting. We did not waste talk at length about idealistic behaviors, or methods that simply do not apply to our specific business. We identified where the team was at, agreed that we had opportunities, and reconciled among each other that a positive change is possible and agreeable to all.

Now, back to preparing for an inspirational meeting. After the meat and potatoes are done, I type up the agenda with the bullet points as presented above and send the agenda out via email 5 days prior to the meeting. This offers everyone time to think about their responses to the questions as they prepare to share their personal thoughts and views with each other. I am not going to name names here, but I want to pose the thought-provoking questions to all team leaders so that they can form their own opinions and be ready to defend their position. It is not until game time that the true intent of the question is revealed.

The detail steps are the fun ones, but they are equally important if you are going to set the tone. I have the middle of the conversation figured out, but I want to get started and end the show with positivity. For an opener, I include a group activity that will involve every person in the room. I usually Google "icebreakers" or group games that focus on the theme of the meeting. If we stay on the topic of 'communication,' I might decide to split the group into two or three teams and play a single round of charades. Some other popular icebreakers include playing darts to tie into the theme of hitting the target or solving a simple jigsaw puzzle to reflect on hiring diverse teams that can work together. Once again, these are behavioral development themes, not for talking about task lists, deadlines or wasting time with grandstanding.

I also want to bring in a list of suggestions that can be done to work on communication on a small level every day. For example, everyone gets assigned to share a story on the group communication board on different weekdays, or we have a contest to submit the best communication-themed meme for our team's break room.

The meeting agenda does not skip out on the opportunity to share task-based issues such as upcoming events or approaching deadlines. However, realize that if your communication is better, all these things will happen in the existing systems. No one wants to just go over a list of tasks in a group meeting. If you do, engagement will absolutely disappear.

As the leader, remember that your role is to introduce the topic, challenge your leaders with questions, and allow the team to come together. If you have ever had to lead a meeting before, I cannot stress enough how important it is to shut up. This is your best opportunity to really observe, listen, coach, and most importantly, discover some new and important perspectives that your team needs you to see. My biggest growth in the meetings comes when I have my listening hat on and not my speaking hat. If you are going to continue to be their leader, first make sure you know who they are and what they are feeling about every issue. Focus on observing and understanding what each person really thinks about communication. You will see who came prepared and who is struggling to keep up. All of these cues will help you take the very best 'next steps' in your coaching.

After the meeting comes a very important step – reflection. We are right back to the heart of this book's most important theme: Discovery. What did you see? Did you learn something new about someone? What would you do differently if you were going to hold the exact same meeting again? How did you perform as the leader? What conversations need to happen next, and do you need to schedule that conversation right now? When you learn to use that meeting as a tool, it can give you so much insight into what your next steps as a leader truly need to be.

If you start having successful meetings, understand how important it is to start leading them from behind. Find a veteran manager, share this method, and put them in a place to lead the next meeting. You are there to support, but you are also there to develop that same mindset, vision, and thought process in your team leaders, one by one. The depth of thought and explosive power of realization is invaluable for spurring your next leader to make their own discoveries.

I will share with you a meeting agenda based on the example in this chapter. Practice creating a similar agenda with whatever topic is most pressing in your current role. Once again, there are substantially more resources, templates, and guides available on our website, by following the QR code here or the link at the end of the book.

Pre-Meeting Communication

1) **Small Wins and Big Accomplishments**
   a) What have you seen over the past month that has caught your attention?
2) **Ice Breaker - Charades**
   a) Best of Three, each member on the winning team gets a $10 Starbucks Gift Card
3) **Common expectations for Communication**
   a) Opening Experience should be well informed
   b) What communication does a great Mid-shift manager do?
   c) Closers are responsible for sharing the results and opportunities
4) **Accountability**
   a) Read & Response times / expectations
   b) Trainers / Trainees / Departmental Meetings
   c) Increasing your communication with your team
   d) A word about Proper Documentation
5) **Challenge Questions**
   a) What benefit do you think shift communication has on our team?
   b) What is the minimum amount of communication you would expect to see from a team member?
   c) Can you think of a time where communication received helped you to avoid an obstacle, or save the day?
   d) What would have happened if you had been blind to that situation?
6) **Group Discussion**
   a) What will our team do in the next 30 days to move forward in your department and managerial communication?
   b) Each manager will need to give an update on planned department meeting dates and details on their specific Area of Responsibility:
      i) Suzy: Growth and Developments in the F&B Department
      ii) Dan: Upcoming events, holiday reminders, vacations
      iii) Charlie: Inventory action items, ordering considerations
      iv) Amanda: Training team, New employee progress
      v) Brad: Recruiting, Hiring, and Interviews
7) **Finally, Employee of the month.**

Who do you think deserves it this month and why?

KEY GOALS IN THIS CHAPTER

- *We celebrate Small Wins every day and celebrate Big Accomplishments every time they happen. The culture of sharing wins is spontaneous and a central theme to any interaction.*

- *Creating conversations that focus on Small Wins & Big Accomplishments creates an atmosphere of positivity and support.*

- *Start by encouraging leaders to come to you with their successes in challenges, and then discuss their newest challenge.*

Small Wins & Big Accomplishments

You may have noticed a section by this name on the Meeting template. Who does not like to brag about themselves a little bit? It feels great to have a moment where you get to share something you feel, saw, or heard that was amazing. There is something very fulfilling about having small successes get noticed, as well as being recognized for major accomplishments.

In *The Last Lecture*, Randy Pausch said,

> *"Showing gratitude is one of the simplest things yet most powerful things humans can do for each other."*

As leaders we often miss golden moments of victory that keep us from giving praise or recognizing something that has happened within your team. When was the last time your team heard you give a round of compliments? When is the last time you heard your team give out compliments to their peers?

At the beginning of each leadership meeting we begin our time with a group share of small wins and big accomplishments that they have seen or achieved. I like to get everyone excited about this moment ahead of time, so the team feels the energy and feels comfortable sharing. This is a key culture piece for us because it accomplishes a lot with little effort.

Sharing Small Wins & Big Accomplishments contributes to increased:

Morale - Everyone gets a chance to share and complement each other.

Awareness – Work can be busy, and sometimes we do not even notice the great things that are happening around us.
Support - When others share the things that give them pride, we get to hear their passion, applaud their effort, and then support them in their future endeavors.
Changing Priorities - Sometimes we are not aware of what is important to someone. Being able to see what your team members are focused on and the personal importance of that goal allows you to rally behind them.
Culture of Sharing – Open sharing creates powerful emotional bonds, responses, and actions. The more we share, the more the entire team becomes accountable for actions that could hurt a team member
Recognition - It is important to recognize key leaders, team members, amazing wins, group wins, and milestones that may have been accomplished in the shadows.
Positive Energy – There may be heavy topics to come, so getting rid of the hang-ups and apprehension early will support real discussion and reduced defensiveness.

When I began implementing the practice of sharing small wins and big accomplishments into our everyday meetings, I witnessed my team change their entire ego. At first, no one wanted to say anything, or would maybe shyly share a proud moment. They soon became a team that was chomping at the bit to unleash a list of things they wanted to share - from small projects they were working on to catching people doing something right. They began sharing how they overcame adversity, how we prepared well for a busy weekend, and so much more.

Beyond that, I saw my team begin passing that same energy down into their department meetings. There are many psychological and emotional benefits in trying to find moments of greatness to share, as opposed to coming into a group session with the intent to complain about struggles. When we celebrate integrity, or going above and beyond in the smallest roles, it is a cycle that keeps giving. We can build a culture reminiscent of the "pay it forward" movement.

It is important to share key moments. Moments are important in both our personal lives and our work lives. Our society has created a culture that tells you not to brag about yourself and what you have accomplished because it may make you look selfish. In the world of social media and online bullies, it is easy to see why people are afraid of sharing anything. If you create a space inside of work where your team leaders are allowed to share their deepest pride, the buy-in to a family and team mindset is tremendous.

Even simple celebration brings energy, togetherness, and a sense of accomplishment that allows your team to feel valued. Data asserts that teams with great cultures are more efficient, deliver more job satisfaction, have reduced turnover, and generate more profit. Happy people accomplish more for their team, they invest themselves more, and dedicate more of their effort to ensure the job is done right.

Realize that in the current job market employees have a buffet of options before them. Between LinkedIn, Glassdoor, and remote job sites, the idea of finding better opportunities without decreasing income can be a tempting prospect. The value of a sense of purpose and recognition cannot be understated in today's climate.

Leaders either feel empowered by development and stay or use your employment to grow a resume. Long gone are the days where people stay in the same career path for 40 years just to earn that Rolex at retirement. Employees must have a reason to choose your team over the competition. The structure of Game Plans gives your team a daily reaffirmation that you are dedicated to their development. Progressive Meetings bring everyone into alignment. Finally, small wins and big accomplishments set the tone for a positive culture dynamic. These resonate with powerful energy to reduce turnover and build veteran leadership teams.

VII

Master Craftsman

KEY GOALS IN THIS CHAPTER

- *Take time to learn every role and the specifics in day-to-day operations that you would expect out of a high performing leader in every space. It is hard to set the expectation if you have trouble demonstrating what 'good' looks like with your own hands.*

- *The true measure of mastery is whether you can teach a task. A Craftsman/Craftswoman is a master of all the skills that compose an operation.*

- *Your personal discovery season should last until you are a master of all the skills it takes to do your job. Do not cheat this process. No detail should be considered too small.*

Know your craft

When you think of the word Craftsman, what things come to mind? Perhaps a finish carpenter, whose intricate detail and arrangement bend your expectations about what is possible with wood and tools. Maybe an architect, who can raise buildings to the sky to stand for hundreds of years. Or maybe a painter, who can reflect beauty and inspire another generation of art students, with only a brush stroke.

Think about the years of attention and practice it takes to find mastery on those levels. It is important to recognize that each smaller step is a skill to be mastered as well. Your path should seek the same detail – master each step along the way, until you have practiced and experienced all the things that will make you great. Just as a fine craftsman creates quality and value for the ages, mastering the idea of Discovery Leadership can create a culture of innovation and development for many generations of leaders to come.

New faces show up fast in a growing company, and Wayne Stancil came to our operation from a similar concept to become our Vice President of Operations. Upon first arrival, he stayed behind the scenes to learn about the mechanics of our company and gather as much information as he could about every person in the company. During a tour of the company, he visited every location we had and took meticulous notes. I have never seen one person take so many notes on a single visit in my professional career as Wayne.

Most of his conversations were simply asking lots of questions, some as basic as "what is the standard font for name tags?" He asked questions for five straight months without saying a lot or leading a meeting in its entirety. Five months and one day later, he finally spoke. When he did so, he spoke with conviction and a complete sense of understanding of what every leader in the company endured, at all levels and locations. His words were accurate, direct, and essential to our growth. Not only did he have his own experience, he knew from our perspectives what each leader knew about the business. Because he took the time to discover our individual strengths and experience, he could truly operate in his role as the Vice President of Operations.

I have also worked for the opposite type of leader who directed without taking the time to truly understand the everyday grind of the business. This made things like respect and motivation hard for those in the "Gemba," where the rubber meets the road day-to-day.

We all respected and understood Wayne, but what made him so effective was his ability to teach you what he saw from the things he had seen through our own eyes. That level of teaching came from developing a craftsmanship that was focused on our unique company and individual leaders.

Taking the time to learn the details of every role means that when it comes time to pave the way forward, this leader can confidently make decisions and hold the respect of the team. To miss out on becoming ingrained in the culture means never getting that initial buy-in and trust of the team. It is difficult to move forward in business if people have any doubts about your ability to understand all the moving parts.

What many leaders fail to do first is master their craft. That is not to say they are not good at their craft, but they have not learned all the intricacies of what it takes to be an effective leader. As one of my favorite anecdotes reflects: "When you teach, you learn twice." First, when speaking, you gain a greater appreciation of the detail when you are forced to explain. Second, you learn exactly the strengths and opportunities of your students. To master any skill, you must teach it.

If you are going to lead others and encourage them, you must first learn the importance and meaning of what you are saying and then speak effectively about it. As you learn the details of your craft you become confident. With confidence comes a vision, and with vision comes blueprints. Notice "blueprints" is plural, because as you lead you will need a series of plans to guide the team to new destinations, as well as individual blueprints for each team leader below you.

Think about the blueprint for your current job. What skills or tasks are required to do your job daily? It could be things like running a cash register, multi-tasking, closing a sale, inventory organization, or attention to detail. Do you feel like you understand the smallest components of the job?

Your personal discovery season allows you to relate to your team leaders and help educate them as they strive to be the best versions of themselves. Your experiences are the key to their success, which is why it is important that your discovery learning is not interrupted. Your ability to go into the metaphorical file cabinet later and dust off your experience at any junction will help you guide and educate a team leader.

Case Study – Consider a Barber's Blueprint

I want you to imagine the process of becoming a great Barber, starting with no skills whatsoever.

The "blueprint" of being a good Barber includes being able to adapt and deliver any customer the hair style they request.

But first, you must understand how to use scissors. Perhaps next you learn to use a trimmer or a razor. You will probably need to know how to clean, sharpen, disinfect, and store all the parts to each. You practice different styles, understand hair types, learn to run a cash register, and so on.

Each one of these steps have taken you closer to mastery, but each one required some time and practice along the way. Now, no matter who walks through the door, their individual hair type, and style requested, you can perform based on the accumulation of skills mastered.

Could you teach someone else how to do your job, from start to finish? If no – what are you missing to become that person?

At some point, could you elevate past this task in the future, now that you have shared the skill set?

KEY GOALS IN THIS CHAPTER

- *As you build your team, teach vision, not just reacting to things as they happen.*

- *Having the answer allows you to help guide the answers. You should not just give answers away.*

- *Seek to discover the components of your team by challenging their thought process with open-ended questions.*

The Chess Master

Many leaders forget the most powerful tool they have in front of them is foresight. Foresight simply means your ability to predict what will happen or will be needed in the future. With experience comes wisdom, but wisdom is only valuable if you use it correctly.

We have all observed managers who "teach" by simply telling people what to do and how to do it. This stifles many bright team leaders because they only learn to react instead of learning how to be proactive. If you find people coming to you for decision-making at the first sign of trouble, you have a lot of teaching left to do. Listening, guiding, and allowing decision making through personal discovery is something I preach to my teams on a consistent basis. To teach vision is a long-term win, and to dictate a path only teaches reaction.

Did you ever have a moment as a child where your parent or guardian insisted you do something "Because I said so!" or that old expression "It's My way or the Highway." Those same expressions may not be explicitly stated but are often implied by the way some people lead their teams. We forget that curiosity leads to discovery, questions lead to discovery, and conversations lead to discovery.

I would challenge you to lead with questions any time you feel like you need to understand an issue. Listen to the challenge that is being shared, and then follow the issue with questions that help you walk through a thought process together. This should lead to a natural and clear conclusion. Finally, ask them what the process will be and the first step towards a solution.

Let us think about how that curiosity and discovery can help you to be successful in a leadership role. During a one-on-one communication session with a leader on your team, you must be open-minded enough to realize a few things:

- Having the exact answer does not mean it always needs to be put on full display. It is not about you; it is about their growth. Giving the answer does not promote discovery for a learner.

- You should be listening to learn something insightful about the other person, to understand their path and how they feel about their role. Listening closely may allow you to hear how they feel/view your leadership and change your own behavior.

- You may find a different way of handling a situation that you would not have thought of. If you are walking into the conversation knowing that you are right, it will close your mind off to better solutions. The most important thing is to know that you could be wrong and that is OK.

It is hard to use foresight if you first do not take the time to get to know your team on an individual and personal basis. You may make decisions, become frustrated, and sometimes write off a person simply because you do not understand their perspective. You are not going to be the one to provide a solution if you do not take the time to solicit their opinions, understand what hurdles they may be encountering, listen to their concerns, or ask what help is needed.!

Many leaders skip this step because it takes time. I will be the first to admit it can consume an entire day or a portion of the day, but I will also tell you that listening to your team is rewarding, inspiring, and invaluable if you are truly passionate about development.

Listening is something that requires attention and asks you to put your ego aside. Once you have allowed yourself to discover the motivations and strengths of your team leaders, let your spirit of coaching open the door to helping them grow. Your previous experiences and scars will allow you the ability to understand what hurdles they may be encountering in that very moment and see the best road ahead. You have to stay present in the moment and solicit their opinions, listen to their concerns, or ask what help is needed. We can use our listening skills to create a teaching moment, a growth moment, or a leadership moment.

Taking one on one time with your team allows your team to start playing chess instead of checkers. Opening their mindset to future results will provide a much clearer path for them to have success. You must spend time figuring out a few key things about your team before you can guide them appropriately. I would recommend putting aside some time on your calendar to ask your team all these questions:

> *What are your aspirations in your personal and professional life?*
> *What short and long-term goals do you have for yourself?*
> *What accomplishment are you most proud of?*
> *What area of responsibility is your strength?*
> *What areas of the business do you need support in?*
> *How would you describe your leadership style?*
> *Who, if any, of your team members would follow you and why?*
> *What are you working on right now?*
> *What do you need from me to support you?*

You can add on or take away from these questions, but the main goal of these questions is to help you gain insight into the person you are leading through. Remember that every team leader will be different, and no one method will work for everyone, so soliciting your team for feedback and understanding is crucial for you to be able to play chess.

More importantly than the answers provided, you should be measuring your own expectations about what role they will play on your team. Let me give you an example:

In my path to discover my own strengths and weaknesses, I am happy to identify that I am not very good at spotting uniform and dress code violations. That is not to say that I do not care about those things, only that I have difficulty in focusing on that behavior when I am observing and coaching. Knowing that, I want to surround myself with people who do well in that skill set.

Asking a Yes or No question is like playing checkers, whereas looking for the motivation and personality behind the answer is the chess mindset. A question with no insight looks like: "is a uniform policy important to you?" During an interview or performance review, I would instead ask the question:

"How do you think personal appearance has an impact on our guest experience?"

The obvious answer to this question is in the affirmation that appearance directly correlates with the guest experience. No customer or guest wants to interact with sloppy, messy, or dirty employees. In most places, the idea of uniformity goes hand in hand with professionalism, and to that end, almost every workplace has standards of practice or general guidelines.

I am not as interested in hearing the checkers answer, "Yes" – I'm listening to the chess answer, the "why" behind their answer. Do they take pride in their personal appearance? Were they raised in an environment where good hygiene was important? Do they believe that all people should be held to similar standards? These are the real and underlying questions that I am trying to solve with their answer. Knowing that I need to surround myself with people who can identify and solve a detail of my business will help me to hire a better team with balanced strengths and weaknesses.

KEY GOALS IN THIS CHAPTER

- *Offering the answers is rarely developmental. Use your conversation time to challenge your leader's choices and reinforce their own decisions.*

- *Every time a question is posed, you can offer a guiding question that will allow the learner to find their own answer.*

- *Your questions should be open-ended, challenging, and asked with the intent of seeking to explain or seeking to understand.*

The Professor

Let me ask you a question – about questions. When a team leader asks you a question, what is your response? Do you respond with an answer right away? Do you tell them to figure it out and come back to you when they have the answer? Do you have them ask someone else or pass the task to another team leader?

When a question is asked, this is when you - the Professor - get to use discovery learning in its fullest. I simply reply with a question of my own.

"What do you think the best course of action is? Why? What have you done before to make you think this way? How did you come to the answer that you just told me?"

I had a team leader who was a rock star in their role as a service trainer. When I made the move to elevate their role to a supervisor, it seemed like all their confidence and self-motivation as a trainer had vanished. I was getting peppered with questions daily about very basic tasks, and I knew it was time to dig deeper into that behavior.

We sat down and talked about the transition from an hourly role to a supervisory role. As a service trainer, they had mastered everything about the functions of the job, and very rarely had an issue pop up that needed outside support to solve. Even when there was a problem, all it took was getting a team leader involved to help make the decision.

We discovered that this new supervisor had never really been forced to make decisions on their own. This happens in so many career paths that the regretful expression "promoted to a level of incompetence" was borne. I promised that our next interaction would be developmental.

Instead of simply providing the decision or instruction, I would challenge them to find their own answer through a series of questions.

It did not take long – later that day, here comes that same supervisor with an issue.

Supervisor: Jeremy, there are four employees in the break room, but only two of them are clocked out on break.
Me: OK, what do you think we should do?
Supervisor: I am not sure.
Me: What does our store policy expect?
Supervisor: That employees in the break room should be punched out.
Me: How do you think their behavior will affect our guests?
Supervisor: They will probably receive poor service because of their lack of attentiveness.
Me: If you are comfortable explaining those things to me, what prevents you from doing the same with those two?
Supervisor: I'm just nervous. I have not had to confront anyone about that stuff before.
Me: I know the guest experience is important to you. The reason you were promoted was to teach your values to others, while learning about our leadership systems. This is a perfect opportunity for you to find a leadership voice and share your expectations for standards, wouldn't you agree?
Supervisor: Absolutely, I did not think about it like that before.

This situation may seem like a no-brainer to anyone accustomed with dealing with leadership issues daily. I had not taken the time to realize that this supervisor had not grown through this experience previously. As the experience level grows, the complexity of the task might become greater, but the method of allowing people to follow a natural path to make decisions never changes.

The first exchange of questions can make the learner nervous and cause them to pause. Some will try to speak on what they believe is the right answer to the question, even if they are not sure of it just yet. Some will come back with, "I do not know," and others will blurt out a halfway thought out answer. I will then ask them to walk me through this process with me because I want them to walk themselves toward the answer on their own terms. Whether or not I already know the answer is irrelevant. The process of discovering this answer with my guidance is the Discovery part.

It is a thrill when I get to help someone on my team get to the solution that they are seeking. Most leaders simply give the answer and move on or tell them to figure it out. It takes much less time to offer the solution without context. There is no teaching or development in those moments. Instead, play chess with your team leader. You know the answer but help them discover and walk them through the process. Anticipate their next move, then have another move in place to redirect them, driving them closer to the answer.

I love this process of leadership because it transforms my team as they go through this question and answer process. It allows them to arrive at the conclusion on their own terms by seeing the growth of their thought process without me just giving them an answer. This process allows them to become independent thinkers. When a problem arises, they already know the process they need to go through to arrive at the solution needed.

After a series of realizations, those who follow the path will even grow into a space where they are able to use the same process while coaching teams under their direct supervision. We now have a second tier of leadership growth happening simultaneously and creating a whole new generation of developing leaders.

Think about your math classes in junior high. For most folks, the process of solving the problem is apparent when the instructor is walking through the steps of solving a math problem on the chalkboard. The real challenge comes with the homework. Separated from the step-by-step instructions, the challenge to solve the problem seems to become so much more complicated.

Let us suppose that the next morning, after struggling with the problem, you went to school early and asked for help in finishing the solution. No math teacher worth their salt would just say, "Well, the answer is X=5". Even though they probably already know the solution, the first step is to make you show your work. What steps have you gone through, where is the point where your problem solving came to an impasse or incorrect step? If the teacher challenges a step in your process, it is to get you to find a better path, correct answer, or easier method. After some amount of changed steps, you have suddenly arrived at the answer to your problem.

This is the pivotal role of a teaching leader. Inspiring your team leaders to find personal development through self-discovery is a tactic that will continue to benefit them for the rest of their lives. When we miss this mark, consider whether you are focused on teaching or more focused on the results. A quality leader is focused on the teaching and knows the results will come.

KEY GOALS IN THIS CHAPTER

- *Stop worrying about yourself. Focus as much time as you can afford on building your team. More importantly, observe and coach those in your shadow to use team-building skills to create another generation of leaders.*

- *If you are only working on yourself, you will also be chasing down new recruits to help you. By focusing on others, you are constantly building a stronger team that cannot wait to support you.*

- *Do not fear redundancy or being replaced.*

- *What things can you give trainees that will allow them to rise into your current position?*

Leadership Shadow

These days, it is very easy to see the similarities between our social media accounts and a leadership mentality. The people around you must see your profile and character, find something to like about your persona, and then subscribe to follow you. Think about that for a minute. Your team must like, follow, and re-post everything about your cultural expectations for you to develop those behind you.

A solid measure of greatness is not how well you are doing, but how well the people in your reflections are doing. That realization was a very difficult lesson for me to realize. Let me share with you a very humbling moment in my career. I was excited heading into a quarterly review because I knew I had done some amazing things recently. Beyond that, I had taken on many new projects, my daily execution was getting much better, and I was getting respect for the results that were coming in. I really felt like I was becoming somebody.

Most reviews are set up like the GPA scale, 1 through 5, however in the professional world you will almost never be a 5. In our company, a 2.9-3.3 is average, 3.4-3.7 should be promotable, and at 3.8 and above you are elite.

My review went exactly like this:

> "Jeremy you have done a great job, and I am immensely proud of your growth and what all you have accomplished. However, in your current role I am not grading you – I am grading your team and their development and what they do when you are not in the building."

My mind was racing, I could not believe the words I was hearing.

"Is this really happening? Is he about to give me an average score after all the energy I put into this job? No way he does that to me...."

And very shortly thereafter, yep, he did give me that sorry 3.2 ranking.

I was not happy about that result because I knew how hard I had worked. This review felt like an indictment of my talent. This was a hard pill to swallow and an even harder concept to grasp. At many times in life you are judged by what you do and what you get done, but when it comes to truly being the leader of a team your results alone can no longer be the focus.

After deep reflection I totally understood what he was saying. Being a solo artist in this profession may allow you to become a famous one hit wonder, but this is not the record business. No self-respecting company built on leadership standards wants a leader that has nothing but selfish intentions. A leader should be able to lead their team to their highest level. Great companies know good leaders never leave behind an empty seat, instead they leave behind a legacy of leaders who continue to develop more leaders to enhance their culture.

People often fear developing their replacement because it makes them replaceable. Imagine having a trusted leader sit down and tell you, "I will teach you enough to be good, but not enough so that I am not needed." That mentality is the very definition of building a glass ceiling. Believe me, if you are building leaders and they hit that limit, they will stop looking to you for guidance and will start looking for a way around you.

The difference is in having a growth mindset and not a fear mindset. A true testament to your ability to be a master craftsman is your ability to develop those around you. The expression can be heard in all different workplaces, "companies pay for leadership," but I think this phrase needs a closer inspection. Companies pay for individuals who align with their core values, create a vision from these values, inspire their team with this vision, and develop competent leaders who can continue to teach the vision in alignment with those same values.

Think about who is directly in your own leadership shadow. One of my favorite exercises to do is a promotion audit. Sit down and ask your shadow the question:

"If you were promoted into my position tomorrow, what part of the role would you struggle with the most?"

Their answer should be very telling. You may hear about a task that they seek mastery on or expose that they have a wide range of skills to work on. No matter what the response is, you have just been gifted with a responsibility that is coming off your plate. The time is now to plan for transitioning that skill – schedule it, guide, and coach the actions, and start developing their own personal mastery of that skill set. One day, you may be responsible for teaching many people to do that same task, simultaneously and across many different buildings. There is no time like the present to start practicing for your next role as well.

There may be a day where the answer to the question of what would be challenging is 'nothing,' but that simply means that it is time to start coaching your leader to do the same activity with their own shadow. The race is never a sprint, it is always going to be a marathon with no end in sight. Be prepared for whatever challenges come up and be available to walk through open doors for a new opportunity. Challenges and transitions are much smoother when there is a distinct leadership shadow standing just behind you.

Even past this discussion, there are a lot of steps in being qualified to say, "I am being paid for my leadership." Do not mistake your loyalty and efforts for leadership. Whether or not your company is aware of this distinction, it is important to ask yourself a very serious question – do I have a leadership role because I'm a hard worker, or because I am a good leader of people? Do not let me fool you, I have fallen into that "hard working" trap more than once or twice in my career as well. It takes a serious amount of effort to pull yourself back into a leadership role once you realize that you have drifted into the place of working just to show that work being done.

Final Discovery

In my first leadership role as an educator, I received advice to avoid being the nice guy. If I wanted good behavior out of my students, I would have to live outside of my natural personality for the first month. When I transitioned into my leadership role at Main Event, I expected the same would be true. However, I found out that adults do not appreciate it when you change your standards, expectations, or systems on a whim. You must start out with authenticity and be comfortable in your own skin. It is important to implement foundations and systems that will allow your team to thrive. You will need to back that up with clear expectations. You do not have to be perfect, but you do have to stay true to who you are. If you do these things you will build trust immediately.

The journey I took was intentional, but I did not know where the path would take me. I did some great work developing some leaders, and I absolutely failed with others – each offering another lesson in Discovery. At the age of 21, 25, or even 30 years old, I could have talked to you about leadership, but I could not have given you tools that you could use on your own. I was still moving through my own discovery and testing my process. I have worked hard to master my tools, and now I would hope to teach you those same skills.

Life is full of ups and downs, and the strength of your team is what will carry you through. This strength begins with the systems you build and the leadership characteristics that define your style. The world will never hear about your great teams if you do not first commit to utilizing progressive, inclusive, and developmental systems. Whether you believe you will achieve greatness or not, you are probably correct.

My hope is that this book provides you with some of those systems to explore with your team – and they in turn use these systems with their own teams down the line. We are not measured by how talented we are, but how far our influence stretches. The tools and game plans in this book executed properly will help you to be a lion leading lions.

Right now is a good time to reflect on what you thought of your role before picking up this book. Every leader and every company is different in so many details that these lessons will look and feel different in your situation. No matter what new tools you decide to implement, remember that you have the ability to define the narrative for a team that will gravitate towards your leadership. Discovery Leadership is centered on the ideal of having the courage to take on new challenges, get to mastery, and then become the coach and mentor that your team needs.

Stay true to your strengths, take time to find them all. Let your Leadership define you. I wish you good luck on your path of Discovery.

About the Authors

Jeremy Mays is a graduate of Mary Hardin-Baylor in Psychology where he focused primarily on helping adults find their purpose while providing assistance on goal setting. He is a certified life coach and public speaker with Extreme Execution, specializing in DISC assessment breakdown. This assessment allows you to see your strongest behavioral style and how to utilize this style to accomplish goals in business, relationships, and life.

He is a General Manager and Assistant General Manager of the Year winner with Main Event Entertainment. He rose from team leader role into General Manager of year by applying the same principles he shares in this book. He is also a General Manager of the year winner and Culture Award winner at Flix Brewhouse. He has established a winning formula that is emulated throughout the company with resounding success.

Matthew Taylor has spent his entire career in the leadership of teams, primarily in F&B operations. After flirting with Electrical Engineering at the University of Texas at Austin, he found a passion in developing leaders in business.

He is an Eagle Scout, Cicerone, trail bike enthusiast, and spent 4 years on the road with new unit openings and guiding a national training team. He is certified by Dale Carnegie Institute for Leading Meetings That Work. His greatest prides include being awarded the Small Business of the Year award by United Way of Central Texas, and his role in constructing the Belton Police Memorial in 2016.

Jeremy and Matthew are co-founders of Discovery Leadership Team, a Leadership training and consulting team based out of Austin, Texas. Discovery leadership Team is committed to growing amazing cultures, developing amazing leaders, and helping those in power become servant leaders.

Our team is devoted to helping organizations form cultures they can be proud of by giving them tools that speak to their leaders.

Online Resources to continue your path

Join us on our official home on the web

www.DiscoveryLeadershipTeam.com

for chapter-by-chapter breakdown of topics presented, printable templates, and exercises. We also offer FREE support with creating your own custom Daily Game Plans, Meeting Agendas, and Team Building Assessments. You can request example packages for corporate speaking engagements and private leadership development coaching via our e-mail address, discoveryleadershipteam@gmail.com

Follow our Social Media platforms for continual updates and support materials

Instagram - DiscoveryLeadershipTeam, #discoveryleadership
Twitter - @DiscoveryLead
YouTube – DiscoveryLeadershipTeam
Facebook Group – Discovery Leadership Team

Made in the USA
Coppell, TX
12 December 2020